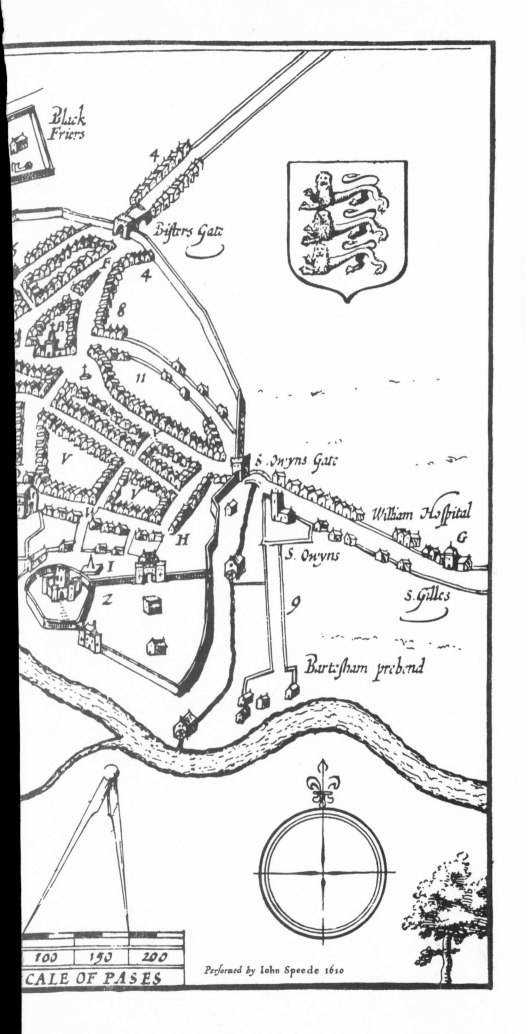

Black
Friers

4

Biſters Gate

F

4

8

11

V

V

V

H

I

A

Z

S. Onyns Gate

William Hoſpital
G

S. Onyns

S. Gilles

9

Bartsham prebend

100   150   200

CALE OF PASES

Performed by Iohn Speede 1610

THE BOOK OF HEREFORD

COVER: High Town in the 18th century, from an original
print reproduced by kind permission of Hereford Library.

Cabbage Lane—David Cox (1783-1859) (Hereford Library)

THE BOOK OF HEREFORD

THE STORY OF THE CITY'S PAST

BY

JIM and MURIEL TONKIN

BARRACUDA BOOKS LIMITED
CHESHAM, BUCKINGHAMSHIRE, ENGLAND
MCMLXXV

PUBLISHED BY BARRACUDA BOOKS LIMITED

BUCKINGHAM, ENGLAND

AND PRINTED IN THIS SECOND IMPRESSION BY

STUDIO TRADE PLATES LIMITED

CHESHAM, ENGLAND

BOUND BY

KEMP HALL BINDERY LIMITED

OXFORD, ENGLAND

JACKET PRINTED BY

CHENEY AND SONS LIMITED

BANBURY, OXON

LITHOGRAPHY BY

SOUTH MIDLANDS LITHO PLATES LIMITED

LUTON, ENGLAND

TYPE SET IN

MONOTYPE BASKERVILLE SERIES 169

BY SOUTH BUCKS TYPESETTERS LIMITED

BEACONSFIELD, ENGLAND

© JIM AND MURIEL TONKIN 1975

ISBN 0 86023 010 4

Contents

Acknowledgements

No book can be written without the help and co-operation of a considerable number of people and institutions.

We are grateful to B. J. Whitehouse and R. Hill of the Hereford Library; Miss A. Barnes, Keith Weyman and F. A. Milligan of the County Library Service; the National Library of Wales; the Library of the University College of Wales at Aberystwyth; Miss E. M. Jancey and her staff at the Hereford Record Office; N. Dove and Miss A. Sandford of the Hereford Museum; the Keeper of the Public Records and staff at the Public Record Office; the Mayor, members and staff of the Hereford City Council.

The book would not have been possible but for the skill and patience of Stephen Jones and Mike Spencer, students of the Herefordshire College of Art, who are responsible for most of the photographic work, both printing and taking. Many of the photographs are from early plates in the Hereford Library Collection taken mainly by F. C. Morgan, Alfred Watkins and Wilson and we are grateful to F. C. Morgan himself and to the library for permission to use them. We are also grateful to L. White, head of the Department of Photography and K. Lindley, Principal of the College, for their help and encouragement to Stephen and Mike. We are also indebted to F. C. Morgan for photographs of the cathedral and chained library and to H. P. Bulmer Ltd., Henry Wiggin & Co. Ltd., Hereford United AFC, Hereford City Council, the City of Hereford Archaeological Committee, the Hereford Library, the Hereford Museum, Miss Gillian Woodhouse, F. R. Boulton, P. A. Rahtz, D. A. Whitehead and the Editors of *The Hereford Times* and *The Shropshire Star & Journal* for help with and permission to use photographs.

Specific acknowledgements are made in the text to the Controller of HM Stationery Office for permission to reproduce Crown-copyright records and to the Mansell Collection.

Finally we wish to thank all those fellow members of the Woolhope Club and other friends in Hereford whose support has encouraged us to write this book.

Foreword

by the Right Worshipful the Mayor of Hereford

We who live in Hereford are reminded every day of our city's past.

The streets we walk were laid out centuries ago and our little stretch of urban motorway passes the walls that protected our citizens in times of trouble. The city escutcheon bears a border of crosses of Saint Andrew that recalls the siege of Hereford by the Scots during the war between roundhead and cavalier, and tourists still trace the trenches and siege-works made by the army that marched away empty-handed in 1645.

This book tells of Hereford's history as a town on a lawless frontier, where the authority of the King was constantly called into question by Marcher-Lord and cattle-thief. It chronicles the growth of civil peace, the development of trade and the growth of our local institutions, and the effect upon the hearts and minds of men of the gentle gospel of Christ as taught by Bishop, priest and monk and witnessed in stone by cathedral, church, chapel and meeting-house. New light is shed upon many incidents in our city's history and many individuals are rescued from oblivion.

Long residence on the border and great skills as archivists and historians have equipped Jim and Muriel Tonkin for their task. They have made effective use of local resources and have had access to much material that was not available to earlier writers. Their book is a fascinating study and worthy of its subject and seems certain to become the standard work on Hereford's history. It will give great pleasure to general reader and specialist alike.

THE CITY OF HEREFORD
July 1975

Mike Prendergast

Preface

by the Chief Steward of the City of Hereford

In 1804 John Duncumb published the first volume of his proposed history of Herefordshire. This contains a long and valuable history of the city of Hereford, and covers many aspects. Since then no important general work has appeared although many guides to the city, and articles upon individual subjects have been published in the transactions of learned societies and elsewhere.

Now, after over 170 years we welcome this new work by Mr and Mrs Tonkin. The authors have both been president of the county archaeological and history society called the Woolhope Naturalists' Field Club, and thus for the first time in a club now 124 years old a husband and wife have in turn occupied this important position. During their time of membership Mr Tonkin has also been editor of the *Transactions* and both have taken a leading part in the study of the history of the city and county. Mr Tonkin is an archaeologist especially skilled in the vernacular architecture of Herefordshire and of Cornwall where he has received important awards. Recently he held a visiting fellowship at the University of Wales. Mrs Tonkin has devoted much of her time to the study of sociology from original sources. Together the authors of this new work upon Hereford have written an authentic and trustworthy account of the history and development of the city and the list of its thirteen chapters show its varied contents.

Those engaged in helping students and scholars to find information upon any subject realize how important it is to be able to suggest a reliable book that does not contain statements copied from earlier and sometimes untrustworthy sources.

I have much pleasure in strongly recommending this volume to all those who are interested in this ancient city which down the ages has played an important part in the history of England.

THE CLOISTERS,
HEREFORD.
April 1975

F. C. Morgan

A Winter's Tale

Why and when are the two questions asked about any settlement; why is it there, when did people begin to live there, what was it like then, what has it been like to live in over the centuries?

We first saw the city from the north on the Canon Pyon road when it was covered in snow, the cathedral tower and the spires of All Saints and St Peter's silhouetted against the whiteness of Dinedor. There it lay, in the Wye Valley with the Black Mountains away to the west. We began to ask ourselves these questions.

The answers to them are under the ground, all around in the streets and in original documents in all sorts of places. This book attempts to answer these questions and to help the 'seeing-eye' to observe the city.

The name itself gives some clue to the origins. It means the 'army ford'; not an army as thought of today, but Old English *here*, a small raiding army. In Anglo-Saxon law it must not be less than twenty-five men.

From these beginnings grew the walled cathedral city, garrison, arsenal and supply base for the Welsh Marches during the Middle Ages. Today it is still an ecclesiastical, administrative and market centre for the Marches, but it has also made parts of Concorde, has the most modern nickel alloy plant in Europe and makes more cider than anywhere else in the world.

The research for this book has been detailed, but the tale is told in such a way that it is hoped it will appeal to the Herefordian who wears a black and white rosette on Saturday afternoon as much as to the scholar. The illustrations are as much a part of the story as the text; together they make up The Book of Hereford.

Ancient arms.

The City

What Structures here among God's Works appear?
Such Wonders *Adam* ne'r did see
In Paradise among the Trees,
No Works of Art like these.
Nor Walls, nor Pinnacles, nor Houses were.
All these for me,
For me these Streets and Towers,
These stately Temples, and these solid Bowers,
My Father rear'd:
For me I thought they thus appear'd.

The City, fill'd with Peeple, near me stood;
A Fabrick like a Court divine,
Of many Mansions bright and fair;
Wherein I could repair
To Blessings that were Common, Great, and Good:
Yet all did shine
As burnisht and as new
As if before none ever did them view:
They seem'd to me
Environ'd with Eternity.

As if from Everlasting they had there
Been built, more gallant than if gilt
With Gold, they shew'd: Nor did I know
That they to hands did ow
Themselvs. Immortal they did all appear
Till I knew Guilt.
As if the Publick Good
Of all the World for me had ever stood,
They gratify'd
Me, while the Earth they beautify'd.

The living Peeple that mov'd up and down,
With ruddy Cheeks and sparkling Eys;
The Musick in the Churches, which
Were Angels Joys (the Pitch
Defil'd me afterwards) did then me crown:
I then did prize
These only I did lov
As do the blessed Hosts in Heven abov:
No other Pleasure
Had I, nor wish'd for other Treasure.

Thomas Traherne (1637-1674)

Before Hereford

Hereford was a Saxon town. Some thousand years before, men settled nearby, at Credenhill —an Iron Age town of perhaps four thousand souls. The Romans, probably driving their roads across the present town's site, preferred lower ground, three miles away at Magnis. But the Saxons first saw the advantages of the site in the seventh century AD, and laid the foundations of today's City. Yet here for centuries past was a safe crossing, a ford over the Wye; here too were some 900 acres of terrace, glacial gravels rising to some forty feet above the river's summertime level, yet in the Bronze Age, earlier man was but a transient— leaving scant traces of his spasmodic settlement in this thickly wooded area, now beneath the western stretch of the later city walls.

The tops of the surrounding hills then, were crowned by Iron Age forts—Aconbury and Dinedor to the south, Sutton Walls to the north and Credenhill to the north-west. This last was occupied from *c* 390 BC until *c* 75 AD—the first town.

The Romans probably built a road from north to south through what is now Hereford; there is a good east-west road of that period forming the present northern boundary of the city. This led from Gloucester to Kenchester (Magnis) about three miles to the west where there was a small Roman town—the forerunner of Hereford. A few Roman remains have been found in today's city, perhaps from Magnis, unless there was a small Roman settlement close to the ford. How much this was used is difficult to say, when there seems to have been a better road and probably a bridge at a point a few miles up the river, leading directly to Magnis.

The road from Viriconium (Wroxeter) via Bravonium (Leintwardine) came down from the north and may have crossed Widemarsh Common to a ford below the site of the present Bishop's Palace. If this road went on to Monmouth, no proof has been found. Certainly a road went south from Magnis to Abergavenny and another to the west to Clyro and Brecon. Thus Magnis was a junction, though the crossing at Hereford may have been used for a short time after the Roman conquest. A few Roman potsherds, some coins and fragments of three Roman altars remain—found where the Victoria Street car park is today. These may well have been spoils from Magnis, or perhaps a small settlement has yet to be proved in the cathedral area.

The Roman town at Magnis suggests a ribbon development along the main east-west road, the north-south road actually being outside the defences. There are two sets of these, the earlier being of mid-second century date and the outer and stronger probably added some two hundred years later with big stone bastions. Houses and what may prove to be a temple have survived, with good tesselated pavements and hypocaust heating.

So Hereford started as an Iron Age town on Credenhill, became a Roman town on lower ground at Magnis, and finally moved to its present site in Saxon times.

ABOVE LEFT: Bronze Age axes found at Fayre Oaks, 1888.

ABOVE RIGHT: Roman altars, Kenchester.

BELOW: Roman pavement, Kenchester.

Saxon City

The first positive evidence of some sort of settled occupation on today's site has been found along the western section of the city walls. A low earth bank and ditch mark the line of a palisade. Beneath this, and therefore earlier, traces remain of two corn-drying ovens, probably of the fifth to seventh centuries AD, but not absolute proof of the settlement.

Cuthbert, Bishop of Hereford from 736-740 and afterwards Archbishop of Canterbury, set up a cross on which he commemorated Milfrith, king of the Magonsaete and three earlier bishops. This suggests that Milfrith, grandson of the last heathen king of Mercia, Penda, and himself a semi-independent king, founded a cathedral city at Hereford, and that makes it one of the earliest in Western Europe.

Clearly by about 700 there was a proper community here, the kingdom of the Magonsaete was incorporated with that of Mercia and the Mercian kings supported the city. Perhaps the first low bank was thrown up around this settlement and may have had its eastern boundary just beyond the cathedral, west of the later castle site.

In 760 the surrounding area was attacked by the Welsh and it is from this early period that the city's Liberty of about 3,500 acres could originate. It is still the administrative boundary of the city.

The first rampart proper was of gravel and clay and was built over the earlier earth bank. The main street of this eighth and ninth century city possibly ran along the line of King Street across the present cathedral site and along the modern Castle Street. This would mean that the early Saxon cathedral—a small wooden building—lay to the south of the present church. Recent excavations have shown that a considerable period elapsed between the throwing up of the low bank and the construction of the first rampart. Perhaps the latter was a defence work against the Welsh in the eighth century, for again there was a considerable time before a much more massive rampart was built.

This must have been part of Aethalfleda's defence against the Vikings in 913-915 with a timber wall at the front and the rear, and the rampart itself laced with large branches. Men from Hereford went out to help repulse the Vikings a few miles to the south of the city and it is classed as a *burh* in the *Anglo-Saxon Chronicle*. In 930 King Athelstan summoned the Welsh princes to meet him at Hereford where he exacted tribute from them.

This massive rampart of the early tenth century included the area now bounded by Victoria Street, West and East Streets and Mill Street—about fifty acres. Inside it was a regular pattern of streets, still the basis of today's plan. Indeed, from St John's Street west to Berrington Street, and the line of Bridge Street and part of Gwynne Street, leading to the central line of St Nicholas and King Streets, virtually preserve the layout of the eighth century Saxon city.

Under Athelstan a mint was set up in Hereford, the only one west of the Severn and there was some settlement outside the defences. (An excavation in 1968 on the line of the defences just north of Bewell Street and another in 1971 west of Widemarsh Street showed this Saxon settlement). A coin of King Canute's reign, *c* 1020 has survived; there is evidence of iron working, including knife-making.

During the episcopacy of Athelstan a new stone cathedral was built; *c* 1050 a castle of Norman type was being built also, by Ralph, Earl of Hereford and nephew of Edward the Confessor. Disaster struck the thriving town in 1055 when the Welsh under Llywelyn ap Gruffydd and Aelfgar attacked and destroyed it. The last stage of the development beyond the walls was destroyed by fire. The interesting feature about this area is that it seems to have been planned with a definite grid of streets and not developed haphazardly. Whether this was in fact extra-mural growth or perhaps even a separate, small settlement as old as the defended area, but which was excluded from the circuit of the ramparts when built in the tenth century, is difficult to judge. Research in other west European towns in recent years has shown similar developments.

Under the new earl, Harold Godwinson, later King Harold of Hastings fame, new defences were built along the line of the later medieval walls, enclosing some ninety-three acres. Archaeological evidence suggests that some of it was built over an area of previous settlement, implying coercion, or fear of another attack. Earl Harold had been given considerable powers and this building of new defences suggests his work. It was from Hereford that he made his great retaliatory invasion of Wales in 1063.

We know from the Domesday Book (1086), that in the Saxon city the king had 103 burgesses. Those who did not have a horse provided guards for the hall when the king was in the city. These burgesses were free and held their *masurae* (burgages or field tenancies), both within and without the walls, at a fixed rent. This reference reinforces extra-mural settlement in Saxon times. There were six smiths and seven moneyers, one of whom was the bishop's moneyer. When the king visited the city they had to coin for him as much money as he willed from his silver. The earl had twenty-seven burgesses who had the same customs as the others. The bishop had ninety-eight burgesses in his fee (property holding). These men probably lived in the twenty-four acres enclosed by the King's Ditch which ran from the river across King Street, roughly along the line of Aubrey Street, to the earlier defences beyond West Street, along the West Street/East Street line to about the junction with Offa Street and then back to the river. North Gate at the northern end of Broad Street was in the Bishop's hands in the thirteenth century. This area is still the parish of St John, which is based on the cathedral, and it is perhaps significant that no public building of importance has been built within it and none at all until 1857. The end of the ditch comes down to the Palace Ford; there are no signs of defences along it and it seems simply to mark a boundary.

We also learn from Domesday Book that the king's burgesses had to work in his fields at Marden for three days during harvest and one day during haymaking wherever the sheriff decided. Three times a year those with horses had to go to the Hundred Court at Wormelow. Each smith paid 1d for his forge and had to make 120 horseshoes from the king's iron, being paid 3d for these. Every man whose wife brewed ale had to pay 10d. Thus ironwork and brewing are two industries mentioned by name in the Domesday account of Hereford.

Recent excavation in Cantilupe Street has shown that the eastern side of the Saxon defences were strengthened by a massive stone revetment in front of the bank, supporting a fighting platform with a retaining wall. This is the first such find in England.

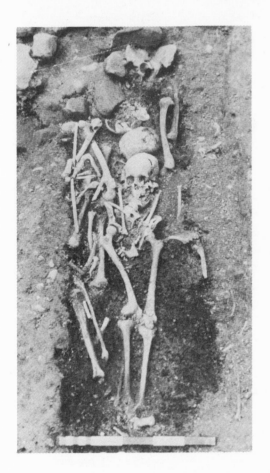

ABOVE: Sixth-century corn-drying kilns and 8th to
11th-century ramparts, Victoria Street. (P. Rahtz)

LEFT: Tenth-century burial, Castle Green.
(Hereford Excavations Committee)

RIGHT: Chester Ware pot, Berrington Street.
(Hereford Excavations Committee)

17

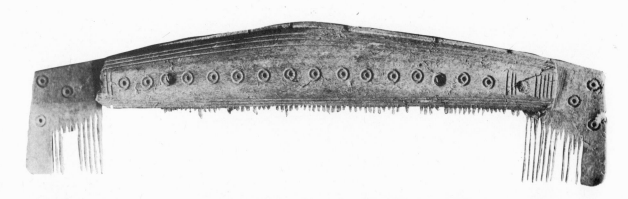

ABOVE: Anglo-Saxon comb. (Hereford Excavations Committee).

BELOW: Eleventh-century Saxon stone wall, Cantilupe Street.
(Hereford Excavations Committee)

18

In the King's Castle

If the fortifications of the city by 1155 enclosed the full ninety-three acres of the area inside today's walls, the market area (modern High Town) was already safely enclosed. The main market area had already moved from Broad Street. The number of the Bishop's burgesses had dropped from ninety-eight to sixty, but other lords, Roger de Lacy and the Lord of Ewyas Harold found it worthwhile to have city property and burgesses. By 1327 according to the *Testa de Nevill* the canons were holding twenty-eight burgages, the Templars one, the Hospitallers seven and the Abbot of Reading thirteen.

Already in the twelfth century the modern parochial boundaries were more or less established—a sign of increasing population. For two hundred years there is constant reference to the walls and the castle. In 1155 there is a reference in the *Pipe Rolls* to the gates of the castle, in 1175 to the battlements and in 1190 to four gates of the city, while in the *Patent Rolls* from 1224 to 1403 at least there are recorded grants to levy tolls towards upkeep of the city walls. Excavation has revealed in the castle a mid-twelfth century church in a graveyard containing burials going back to Saxon times and an earlier building, possibly also a church. Quite probably the later church is St Martins 'in the king's castle' which Hugh de Lacy gave to the monks of St Guthlac's *c* 1180.

The growth of the castle was a help to Hereford and encouraged the city's increase in size and wealth. Early in John's reign, 1202 and 1203, work was in train on the gates, and by the 1240s on a small tower. Mention is made of a great tower which was reroofed in 1402, when seven of the ten semicircular watchtowers were built.

Some idea of its size and importance in 1265 is given in a *contrabreve* to the sheriff to 'fit the tower of Hereford castle with joists and roof it with lead; to make a bridge to the tower, repair the king's and queen's halls, chambers and kitchens, the larder, the knight's chambers, the king's chapel, the stable and two turrets; to finish a chamber lately begun for the king's clerks; to make a bakehouse, to repair the walls descending from the tower to the city and the Wye; to repair the king's hall belonging to the almon(ry), the halls where the county courts are wont to be held, the Exchequer chamber in the castle, the wall round the castle and the towers in the inner bailey; to make a building for housing the engines, the gate beneath the tower, the swing bridges there, and a prison within the castle . . .'. Perhaps the 'sixty oaks from the king's haye' taken for repairing the castle in 1267 were a result of this. From a similar document of 1249 it is known there was also 'the king's grange' (barn) in the castle, and money was spent in that year and in 1240 on the 'new tower'.

The order in 1233 'to cause a fair and becoming chapel of the length of twenty-five feet to be made at the end of the oriel in the king's chamber in Hereford castle and to cause it to be wainscotted' is one of the earliest known references to an oriel (oriolli), a vestibule giving access from one apartment to another. The timber was to come from the bailiwick of Hugh de Kilpec.

We cannot be sure, what the houses of the town were like in the early medieval period, but in 1267 Sarah the Jew and her son Jacob sold a 'messuage and all the houses, stone and timber thereof'. This implies a stone house of the type found in Lincoln and Bury St. Edmunds. Certainly in Eign Gate, just west of All Saints' Church, there is a stone cellar and the groining which remains suggests a fourteenth century building. It is the oldest known surviving remnant of a stone domestic building in the city. An interesting light on life at the time is thrown by the various rents paid: one clove, one peppercorn, one rose, a pair of gloves valued 1d, one pound of pepper, one silver penny and, for a lease of lands, 'ten loads of corn well dried, winnowed and measured'.

Outside the walls the city had grown on the north and east and across the Wye, but perhaps not much on the west. In 1265 a scorched earth policy prevented rebel barons using the suburbs, and in the file of *Miscellaneous Inquisitions* there is a description of burning in the suburbs including the 'house of Aylmeston'. There were extensive open fields to the north—Widemarsh Port Field—and to the east—Prior's Port Field, where the burgesses and corporate bodies held arable strips intermixed.

In 1395 an enquiry was set up as to what persons had built on the road to the castle where the corn market had long been held. It is clear from the *Patent Rolls* that this was adjoining the bridge and fosse of the castle, proving that the corn market was in the area east of the cathedral at that time.

The castle prison was used to house a murder accomplice in 1346 and in 1453—another of the cathedral muniments mentions the 'Barbigan' which was three perches and two feet from the river. John Leland, visiting the city in 1538 estimated that 'the castel . . . be of as great circuite as Windsore'.

A number of houses from the later medieval period survive in the city, sufficient to show what it must have been like. Some have a hall or main room on the first floor, all were timber-framed, many of them jettied, and the great majority were built at right angles to the streets with a long passage-way down the side leading to the yard or garden at the rear. The upper storeys were built out over these passage-ways. Many houses had cellars, some of them elaborately vaulted; it is interesting that many of these are back from the present street line and there seems to have been sixteenth and seventeenth century encroachment on to the streets.

In the 1660s some idea of the city can be obtained from the Hearth Tax returns. Altogether tax was paid on 364 houses, counting the College of the Vicars Choral as one. This excludes the smallest, (houses worth less than £1 a year). The largest number in one ward was 118 in Bysters, (the Commercial Street area). The locales with the biggest houses appear to have been St Owen's Ward, which included the Cathedral and Castle Street, and Wigmarsh Ward, the Widemarsh Street area. There less than half the houses had only one or two hearths; in the other parts of the city about two-thirds did. Many of these houses still survive, most refronted in brick, some in stone; their fine timber-work, panelling and decorated plaster ceilings are a token of the prosperity of pre-Civil War Hereford.

About this time the castle suffered badly, for in 1645 the keep was razed, two years later Robert Harley bought it from John Birch for £600 'for publique use and benefitt' and in 1652 much of the stone was sold for building the new hall of the Vicars Choral and the Tolsey. In the following century the Society of Tempers became the tenants of the castle under the county magistrates in whose care it had been placed. It looked after the green, trying to keep the castle area in decent repair.

Defoe spoke of Hereford in 1725 as being 'mean built and very dirty', probably a result of poor transportation, little native industry and its narrow, medieval streets. However, in 1697 Dr Brewster had built his fine, up-to-date house in Widemarsh Street where its good proportions and elegant cornice still catch the eye today. Recent excavation has shown the formal garden layout of Bewell House and in the St Martin's area Drybridge House had been built before 1734. All these are of brick; Hereford was beginning to get over its period in the doldrums.

Late in the century the gateways were taken down—Wye Bridge and Friars in 1782, St Owen's, 1786, Eign, 1787, and Bysters and Widemarsh in 1798, thus opening up the streets. The hospital was opened in 1783, the Duke of Norfolk built his fine town house at the top of Broad Street in 1790—it became the City Arms in 1794—and John Nash's gaol followed in 1796. In spite of a comment in 1784 that its appearance was 'melancholy and monastic' Hereford was beginning to acquire a new face. St Owen's Street and St Martin's Street were good provincial Georgian streets. The changes continued, for in 1818 part of the Butchers' Row occupying the middle of High Town was taken down and after further public subscription the remainder of it in 1837, leaving only the 'Old House'.

The Bridewell, the last remaining building of the castle was sold for £500 in 1800 and still remains as a private house. The Society of Tempers did their best by the Castle Green until 1831, and finally it was let in 1873 to the city for 200 years at £1 per annum. Since 1882 it has gradually been laid out to take its present form; the Victoria Suspension Bridge linking it with Putson meadows opposite, was erected in 1897.

A glance at the street names will show the expansion during the last hundred and twenty years and the coming of the canal, 1845, and railway, 1854.

In 1833 the city was described as being 'tidy and proper', by 1861 it was 'built of brick, neat and cheerful'. Many of the old streets and lanes were renamed in 1855, but it was not until 1908-11 that some seventy old houses in the Bewell, Friars and Cross Street area and Turk's Alley were demolished. Land north-east of the station was bought and laid out as the 'Garden City'. Hereford had entered the field of municipal housing.

The city's population in 1901 was 21,382 compared with 6,828 a hundred years earlier; in 1931 it was 24,163 while in 1971 it had risen sharply again to 46,950. The two great periods of growth have been 1851-71 and the 1950s and 1960s. Even so the *Subsidy Rolls* gave Hereford as the thirteenth town in England in 1334 and nineteenth in 1377: it has dropped down the league table since then. It was still nineteenth in the 1520s, but a hundred and forty years later its number of taxable hearths was 1,099 whereas Chester in nineteenth place had 3,004. For the past three hundred years Hereford has not been one of England's great cities if sheer size is a criterion.

Hereford entry in Domesday Book, 1086.
(By permission of the Controller of H.M. Stationery Office).

ABOVE: Thirteenth century pottery from Offa Street, 1957.

BELOW: Murage grant, 1298, by Edward I.

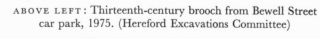

ABOVE LEFT: Thirteenth-century brooch from Bewell Street car park, 1975. (Hereford Excavations Committee)

BELOW LEFT: Fifteenth-century fireplace, Acacia House, Putson.

CENTRE ABOVE: Fourteenth-century vaulting, Old Greyhound, Eign Street, 1923.

CENTRE: Model of city as it was *c* 1640 by J. L. Starkey.

CENTRE BELOW: City Wall on west side, 1975, showing bastion.

24

ABOVE LEFT: Freeman's Prison, *c* 1600, demolished 1939.
ABOVE RIGHT: Early 17th-century gable, High Street.
BELOW: Seventeenth-century panelling, St Owen Street.

ABOVE LEFT: Widemarsh Gate, taken down 1798.

ABOVE RIGHT: Sixteenth-century manor house, Putson.

BELOW: View of Hereford, 1775, Francis Grose (1731-91).
(Hereford Museum)

27

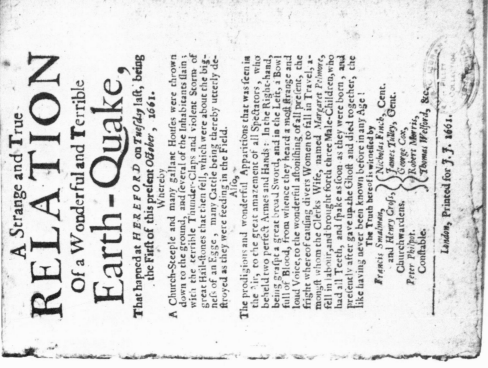

LEFT: Hereford earthquake, 1661.

RIGHT: Seventeenth-century room, Green Dragon Hotel.

28

Bysters Gate, taken down 1798.

ABOVE: Butcher Row, from sketch by David Cox, 1814.

BELOW: Cooken Row (in High Town).
(Hereford Library)

ABOVE LEFT: Broad Street and All Saints Church, pre-1778.

ABOVE RIGHT: Belmont Road, looking north-east, 1940.

CENTRE RIGHT: Ross Road—Belmont Road junction, 1940.

BELOW: North-east side of St Martin's Street, 1825,
where Norfolk Terrace now stands.

31

ABOVE: Eign Street, looking east *c* 1900.

BELOW: Bottom Broad Street.

Chapter and Verse

Whatever gods men worshipped locally, their devotions date back at least 1800 years. Then Roman townsmen worshipped at any one of three altars, but where those altars stood, no one knows. That there must have been a Roman temple either at Kenchester or within the site of today's city, is certain, for those same Romans left fragments of all three altars behind at Victoria Street.

Some time during the next four centuries Christianity came to Hereford which rapidly developed as a diocese in its own right.

Cuthbert, later Archbishop of Canterbury, was Bishop of Hereford, 736-740, and he lists three predecessors from 676 one of whom, Walkstod is described by Bede as the bishop west of Severn. Walkstod's wooden cathedral was almost certainly here. It seems that a diocese was set up by Milfrith, King of the Magonsaete, and that it received the support of the Mercian kings when they incorporated the smaller state into the kingdom. In fact, a bishop of Hereford is listed as one of the seven British bishops who met St Augustine in 601, but he may have represented a western Celtic Christian community rather than one based on the city. In 669, Putta, Bishop of Rochester, whose own diocese had been overrun, came to the area, but there is no proof that he was ever Bishop of Hereford.

In 792, Ethelbert, the young king of the East Angles, was murdered, probably on the orders of Offa, and his body was eventually brought to Hereford and buried there. Miracles were worked at his tomb, especially the curing of paralysis; the cathedral had acquired a saint whose relics were to benefit it especially in the twelfth and thirteenth centuries. The dedication to St Mary at some later date became St Ethelbert and St Mary.

As early as c 1006 the Anglo-Saxon will of Wulfgeat of Donnington in Shropshire leaves 'to St Ethelbert's the equivalent of half a pound; and to St Guthlac's the equivalent of half a pound'. The dedication to Ethelbert was clearly established by that date.

A twelfth century record suggests that a stone cathedral may have been built in the ninth century, but the first certain record is of a new stone church erected during the time of Bishop Athelstan, 1012-1056, which was destroyed by the Welsh in 1055 when seven canons were killed attempting to prevent the soldiers from entering.

The destruction appears to have been complete and a new Norman building gradually took shape between c 1080 and c 1140, being consecrated in the presence of six other bishops between 1142 and 1148. Much of this building still remains, especially the great arcades. The cathedral was designed for aisle towers, as in Charlemagne's great church at Aachen and a rare feature in England, the northern one at least apparently having been built and taken down at a later date.

Gradually the great church grew and changed, the beautiful Early English Lady Chapel being completed c 1225, the clerestory of the choir and its vaulting by c 1240, the north transept by c 1268 and the inner part of the north porch c 1255.

Already the cathedral had had some characters of national importance. In 1101 Gerard had been translated to York, Gilbert Foliot, 1148-63, had become Bishop of London and under William de Vere, 1186-1200, a circle of great scholars was assembled at Hereford including Walter Map, Giraldus Cambrensis and Robert Grosseteste, later Bishop of Lincoln. Both Hugh Foliot, 1219-34, and Peter de Aquablanca, 1240-68, fought for the rights of the church against the city and the latter, who was chiefly an ambassador overseas for Henry III, was responsible for the building of the north transept on the model of Westminster Abbey.

During these years the Bishop and cathedral clergy jealously guarded the rights acquired over many years. One important step in this was a Papal Bull of 1135-6 confirming the grant of possessions by *Meredith* (Milfrith) *King of the English*, four hundred years earlier. The Bishop and the Chapter did not always agree, each side attempting to preserve its privileges. In 1180-86 the Bishop had to order the Dean and Chapter to remove the archdeacon's house from the burial ground of the cathedral. In 1399 Aquablanca was ill overseas and the canons wrote enquiring after his health, one suspects very much tongue in cheek. They were disappointed; the bishop replied that he was returning as soon as possible.

When Gilbert Foliot was Bishop, 1148-63, there is definite notice of the endowment of prebends and in 1198 Richard I granted land for the improvement of the canons' commons, these being the provisions and certain privileges they received in common. Almost a hundred years later there is a long list of the sums distributed to the canons according to the services they had attended. In 1175 Dean Jordan gave land to brew beer for the canons and about the same time David de Aqua made provision for the annual distribution of simnel cakes.

The cult of St Ethelbert seems to have reached its climax about this time, the story having been built up by William of Malmesbury (who stated in 1141 that his relics were in the cathedral) and by Geraldus Cambrensis. It is perhaps significant that in 1131 it was said that there were no notable relics in the cathedral, but no doubt money left at the shrine helped to build and maintain the great church.

From time to time there are references in the cathedral muniments showing the workings of the chapter. In 1270 they agreed to send one-twentieth of their goods and chattels to help finance a crusade, and in 1286 fifteen bags in an iron chest contained £1,222 4s 6d of old money, which was taken to London as the tenths collected for the Holy Land. In 1302 a receipt for 24s recorded payment for oil for use in the cathedral.

The Consuetudines of the Cathedral, the Hereford Use, was to a large extent unique. These and the Statutes of York show no verbal agreement with those of Sarum which were the model for most of England. One interesting feature is the enrichment of this use by the feasts of women saints eg Anne, Katherine, Lucy, Mary Magdalene and Milburga.

Probably from the twelfth century the cathedral has been the base for the parish of St John and a parish church has been situated in various parts of it from time to time.

Then in 1274 Thomas Cantilupe became bishop, dying in Italy in 1282. His bones were brought back and buried in his cathedral. Soon it was reported that miracles were being worked at the tomb in the Lady Chapel and in 1287 Edward I was present when the relics were moved to the north-west transept. Great wealth was obtained from the pilgrims and was used to rebuild the central tower, the north transept aisle and tomb for Cantilupe and the nave aisles. In 1290-91 there were fifty masons working on the cathedral. As early as 1285 the Bishop of Worcester was granting indulgences to pilgrims to the tomb of Bishop Thomas, and Richard Swinfield, Cantilupe's successor, was soon petitioning the Pope for canonisation. Finally in 1307 an inquiry was held which lasted from August to November.

The six commissioners headed by two bishops examined in the fullest detail 115 witnesses of seventeen miracles and altogether collected written details of 221 miracles. One of the methods of effecting a cure was by 'measuring to St Thomas' using thread with which candles were made. Considerable quantities of silver vessels, wax, gold and silver rings and brooches, garments of gold thread and silk given by the cured as well as crutches left by them were exhibited. The principal cures seem to have been of paralysis and restoring those who had died by drowning. In 1320 St Thomas was canonised and in 1349 his remains were transferred to a magnificent shrine in the Lady Chapel.

In 1320 a goldsmith had been paid £10 for work on this shrine, and a year later a further £10 (part payment of £40) was paid for marble. In the same year £80 was paid for electrum (an alloy of gold and silver) for the tomb. St Thomas received a worthy resting place.

All the new work had been carried out on the old foundations and Adam de Orleton, 1317-27, had to appeal for funds to secure them. The pilgrims provided the money, the foundations were secured and the cathedral was left very much as we see it today except for the west end. The towers and several of the tombs carry the ball-flower ornament, Hereford showing more of this rich, early fourteenth-century detail than any other building in the country.

The beautiful chapter house was built next but destroyed in the seventeenth century and the cloisters were being built during most of the later part of the fourteenth and early fifteenth centuries, probably replacing earlier ones of wood.

Contracts are still extant between the dean and chapter and John of Evesham, mason, in 1359, and from five years later with Thomas of Cambridge, mason, who agreed to finish his work on the chapter house within seven years.

In 1372 Wycliffe had made his attack on the friars and Herefordshire came under some Lollard influence. During the next ten years Nicholas de Hereford was working on an English translation of the Bible, but later made his peace with the church, becoming chancellor of the cathedral in 1391. Two years later Walter Brut was tried at Hereford before the bishop and forced to recant.

There is an occasional record of gifts bequeathed to the cathedral. One in 1361, among many other things included a pontifical ring, none of its stones being missing, and in 1371 the dean was left 'a mitre of spotted red velvet with eagles of white pearls and silver plates enamelled at their circumference'.

Excommunication was a frequent punishment for a number of offences, serious and otherwise. It was used in Bishop Aquablanca's time to deter the citizens of Hereford, in one of their frequent quarrels with the church over control of certain aspects of the city's trade. Again, in 1386 those who had killed and stolen the swine of master John de Erle were excommunicated.

The vineyard of the dean and chapter, one of a number in the county, was in 1463 leased along with 'a building called le logge and a columbarium' and 'the fishery within that part of the Wye' 'near Lutteley'.

Two beautiful chantry chapels were built both with well-executed fan-vaulting: Stanbury's between 1480 and 1490 and Audley's c 1500. The addition to the porch by Richard Mayew, 1504-16, who had earlier built Magdalen tower, Oxford, and Charles Bothe, 1516-35, was completed by c 1519 and was the last part of the cathedral to be erected before the Reformation.

A covered walk with a beautifully carved roof leads from the cathedral to the college of the Vicars Choral which was built between 1472 and 1475 to house the twenty-six vicars and the custos. This replaced their earlier building in Castle Street which they had complained was 'so distant from the church that through fear of evil-doers and the inclemency of the weather, many of them cannot go to the church at midnight to celebrate divine service'. There was an endowment for six vicars as early as 1237 and they were granted incorporation as a college in 1395 by Henry IV. They were reduced to twelve in 1637 and then to four in the nineteenth century. Their houses in the close, each of two rooms one above the other, have been converted into homes for diocesan officials, and still look much as they must have done five hundred years ago. Part of the finely carved roof of their fourteenth-century hall in Castle Street still survives in a private house.

A great timber palace for the bishop was built c 1180 between the cathedral and the river —not so much a house as a magnificent hall for official gatherings. Today it still stands, with its massive timber posts and arches with nail-head ornament, but cased in brick, one of three or four surviving great Norman aisled halls in England.

There were five parish churches in the medieval city: All Saints, St Nicholas, St Peter within the walls and St Martin's and St Owen's outside. There were also houses of the Black and Grey Friars, the Knights Templars and the Knights of St John beside the priory of St Guthlac's and a chapel of St Martin in the castle. The original St Guthlac's, founded as a collegiate church by King Athalbald, 716-57, on a site within the later castle area, was moved outside the walls by Bishop Robert de Bethune, 1131-48; now the hospital and 'bus station in Commercial Road occupy the site. In 1436, besides considerable possessions outside the city, it owned seventy-one tenements, seventeen gardens, two mills, two barns and two shops in the city as well as a close, two crofts and across the river in St Martin's, the 'Kyngisorchard' of ten acres.

The Grey Friars (Franciscan) were established in Hereford by 1250 and seem to have had no troubles with either city or church. Their church and conventual buildings lay between Barton Road and the river, just west of St Nicholas car park. There is no trace of them today, but during the First World War allotment holders found some scanty remains and part of a thirteenth-century doorway.

The story of the Black Friars (Dominican) in Hereford is much different. They were given some land in the Portfield outside St Owen's Gate in 1246 and ten oak trees from the Forest of Dean towards their buildings. They were strongly opposed by the cathedral clergy, who felt there were quite enough charities to be supported in the city without adding another. In fact, they probably feared that less money would be attracted to the cathedral. In spite of warnings from the Pope in 1250 and 1254 the friars persisted in their attempt and although they received letters of protection from the King in 1270, it was not until c 1319 that they were granted a new site outside Widemarsh Gate under the patronage of Edward II. The scanty remains which were much altered in the seventeenth century are behind Coningsby's Hospital in Widemarsh Street. Beside them still stands their beautiful red sandstone cross, the only one of its type surviving in England.

Both the great orders of religious knights had buildings just outside the walls. The Templars had a round church, like that still surviving in Cambridge, in St Owen Street a little to the south of where St Giles Chapel now stands. Its foundations were discovered in 1927 when the second chapel, built in 1682, was demolished for road widening. On the west wall of St Giles almshouses is preserved an elaborate stone carving of Christ in Majesty, typical of the best work of the 12th century Herefordshire school of carving. The Hospitallers had a cell founded by Henry II near the Black Friars, where Coningsby's Hospital stands today. In 1505 they owned some ninety tenements in the city, worth £6 13s 5½d.

All these religious houses were dissolved at the Reformation, and the Templars long before that, but the parish churches survived, only to have two of their number, St Martin's and St Owen's destroyed by the Scots in 1645. A new St Martin's was built in 1845, but farther out from the walls than its predecessor. St Owen's parish was combined with St Peter's.

The latter was founded soon after the Conquest as a Collegiate Church richly endowed with lands in Herefordshire and Shropshire. Its founder, Walter de Lacy, was killed in 1085 by falling from its battlements, and his son, Hugh, gave it in 1101 to the Abbey of St Peter at Gloucester, making it a priory. Thirty years later Bishop Robert de Bethune moved St Guthlac's from the castle to its new site and combined the priory of St Peter with it. Thus the building had been collegiate church, priory and then parish church all within thirty years. So it still remains.

At the other end of the market area, with another spire just as conspicuous as St Peter's, is All Saints. It is a fine thirteenth-century church with much later work. Here again is some of the wealthy ball-flower decoration, this time on a piscina in the chancel and, unusually for Herefordshire, there is a hammer-beam roof in the north aisle. All Saints possesses the second biggest chained library in the country, the biggest being in the cathedral. Most of it was given to the church by the will of Dr Brewster in 1715. In the mid-nineteenth century a churchwarden sold this rare collection of 326 books to a dealer for £100, but fortunately the Dean of Windsor, who was the patron, and the bishop, heard of it in time to prevent the books leaving the country.

The church of St Nicholas survived the Civil War, though with considerable damage, was much restored in 1718, but in 1841 was taken down and a new church built just outside the walls in 1842.

Like the cathedral these medieval churches had gifts of money and property left to them for the setting up and maintenance of chantries, and in the muniments there are occasional references to these, as in 1355 when we read of 'a tenement in Wybruggestret pertaining to the perpetual chantry of Walter de la Barre in the church of St Nicholas'.

Hereford was not really in favour of the Reformation. Bishop Scory, a reformer who was consecrated in 1559, did not get on well with his clergy, complaining that there were no butchers open on the Vigil and Feast of the Assumption and writing to Cecil in 1561 to the effect the 'Popish Justices' were impediments to religion.

It does seem that some of the cathedral clergy were not all they should have been, and in 1582 a commission was appointed which drew up a code of Statutes relating to qualifications, behaviour, the library, the school, preaching and other matters including the cathedral property. These were revised again in 1636 in a less Puritan fashion, much nearer in spirit to the medieval 'consuetudines', and still continue as the code of the Chapter of Hereford.

During this period, one of the canons, Miles Smith was working as the principal translator of the Authorised Version of the Bible leaving his Hebrew and Arabic books to the Cathedral when he died in 1624. The library of which these form part is one of the Cathedral treasures today.

The organ was built in 1686 by Renatus Harris, a famous organ builder, and was added to in 1806, 1862 and 1908. Originally it stood on the stone screen which has been removed, then at the east end of the north aisle, and in 1862 arrived at its present position.

On the whole the city did not persecute non-conformists too severely, though there must have been much unpleasantness of which we can learn little today. One martyr was John Kemble, a Herefordshire-born priest who was executed on Widemarsh Common on August 22, 1679, at the age of eighty. He asked the executioner if he could have a last pipe; the request was agreed and they sat and smoked together.

37

Earlier evidence of recusants occurs in 1585 when a number of books were seized, and in the citing of Richard Ravenhill in 1639.

One custom deriving from the pre-Reformation mysteries went on in Hereford until 1706 and was unique in England. It was known as the Hereford Riding when a labourer rode a donkey into the city during Passion week.

During the Commonwealth, the Cathedral Clergy lost their posts, though many retained other livings elsewhere. The cathedral was staffed by 'preachers', most of whom had held livings in the diocese before this; at least two became licensed non-conformist preachers in 1672.

On the whole the cathedral did not suffer much during the Civil War, both Colonel Birch and his aide, Captain Silas Taylor, restraining the soldiers from doing much damage. The great loss was the chapter house. Lead from the roof is said to have gone to make bullets during the siege, and in 1646 to repair the castle roof, and its stone was used in the rebuilding of the palace by Bishop Bisse in 1720. The other important part, pulled down by Bishop Egerton in 1737, in spite of the protests of the Society of Antiquaries, was the early Norman upper and lower chapel of St Katherine. Based on the chapel of Charlemagne at Aachen, it stood to the south of the cloisters as the bishop's chapel.

On Easter Monday, 1786, the west tower and west front of the cathedral collapsed. James Wyatt restored the cathedral one bay shorter than previously and took down the central spire. The work was finished in 1797; but Wyatt's executors were not finally paid until 1817.

During the rebuilding the bishop was John Butler. He wrote to Lord Nelson, when the latter visited Hereford in 1802, that on account of age and infirmity he could not pay his respects to his Lordship—to which Nelson replied that he would call on him at the palace.

The stone choir screen was pulled down in 1840 so that reconstruction work could be carried out on the tower. It was the last in England to stand under the western arch of a central tower and was not replaced, a new metal screen being erected by Sir Gilbert Scott in 1864 under the eastern arch. This in its turn was taken down a few years ago.

In 1907 this new west end was in its turn replaced. Thus the building we see today is not really much different from that of five hundred years ago.

With the growth of the city, further new churches were needed outside the walls, St Paul's being built at Tupsley in 1865, St James in Green Street in 1865 and Holy Trinity at Whitecross in 1883 as a chapel to All Saints, becoming a parish church in 1902.

Other Christian sects set up places of worship in Hereford. As early as 1660 twenty-three Quakers were molested and arrested at a meeting at Hinton and there is a continuous record of their sufferings until the Act of Toleration in 1689 when they registered their meeting house in the 'city suburbs without Fryne Gate'. This building, in Quakers' Lane, continued 'though seldom used' so it was said in 1796, until 1822 when the present one was built in King Street.

Also in 1796 the Dissenters 'have a Meeting-house without Eignegate, and a good house and garden for the Minister'. This is now Eignbrook United Reformed Church which was replaced in 1829 and again by the present building in 1873. This is probably the oldest continuously active non-conformist body in the city, for in 1656 William Peyton is described as 'minister at Barton'. It was certainly founded by 1662 and George Primrose, one of the cathedral preachers during the Commonwealth, seems to have been the minister, being succeeded by John Weaver who was so severe that his flock dwindled to a handful. A church at Wyebridge seems to have been used from 1707 until the building of that at Eignbrook. In earlier writings the congregation is sometimes described as Presbyterian, though later on this sect had a church of its own in Hampton Dene Road, now a second United Reformed Church.

The Roman Catholic parish of St Francis Xavier was established in 1684, the present church in Broad Street having been built in 1838-9 on a site which had already been occupied by its predecessor since 1792. Its most precious possession is a relic of John Kemble. The church of Our Lady Queen of the Universe has recently been built in Belmont Road.

In 1793 Lady Huntingdon's Connection had a place of worship built in Berrington Street, described in a contemporary directory as a chapel of the Calvinistic Methodists and in 1796 as 'a very neat chapel of the Methodists'. It is now a bingo hall. In 1887 the Connection built a new church at Crozens, Eign Road.

Significantly, it was not apparently until 1792 that any religious body other than the established church had its place of worship inside the city walls.

The Wesleyan Methodists had a chapel in 1821, and by 1829 had built the now disused chapel in Bridge Street which was given its stone front in 1866. The present Christadelphian Church, Holmer Road, was built as a Wesleyan Chapel in 1876.

The Primitive Methodists had a place of worship in Union Street by 1826 and their Ebenezer Church, now disused, was built just outside St Owen's Gate in 1838. The Clifford Street chapel, now two cottages, followed in 1867, while the present day Methodist Churches in St Owen Street and Chandos Street were both built by the Primitives, in 1880 and 1902 respectively, replacing the two earlier and smaller buildings.

Strangely enough the Baptists seem to have been late in arriving in Hereford, becoming established in Commercial Road in 1829 as Zion Chapel, now disused. Their present Church in the same road was built in 1880 and there is another at Putson.

Today the Christian Brethren, established in the city in 1829 as the Plymouth Brethren and moving to their present building in Barton Road in 1859, the Apostolic Church, 1912, the First Church of Christ, Scientist, Church of God, Elim Pentecostal Church, Jehovah's Witnesses and, most recent arrival, the Church of the Latter Day Saints (Mormons), all have places of worship in Hereford.

The Salvation Army citadel is in Maylord Street in the area once occupied by the Jewish Community which has met on some recent occasions in the Quakers' Meeting House. Not for the first time in the city's history Jews and Christians have got together, for in 1286 a number of Christian guests attended a Jewish wedding at which there were equestrian and theatrical performances, sport and minstrelsy—and were excommunicated for doing so.

Hereford Cathedral, 1794, J. M. W. Turner. (Hereford Museum)

ABOVE LEFT : St Ethelbe

BELOW RIGHT :

CENTRE : Early 13th-century

ABOVE RIGH

BELOW LEFT : C.

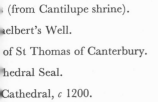

(from Cantilupe shrine).

elbert's Well.

of St Thomas of Canterbury.

hedral Seal.

Cathedral, *c* 1200.

41

ABOVE: Papal Bull, 1135.

BELOW LEFT: Cathedral, Norman choir. (F. C. Morgan)

BELOW RIGHT: Cathedral, Early-English Lady Chapel.

Page from Hereford Use, *c* 1265.

Mappa Mundi, *c* 1300.

44

ABOVE LEFT: Capital in Bishop's Palace, c 1180.

ABOVE RIGHT: Roof of Corridor to College of Vicars
Choral, late 15th century.

BELOW: Monument of St Thomas Cantilupe, 1282.

45

ABOVE LEFT: Twelfth-century tympanum of
Christ in Majesty, St Giles.

BELOW LEFT: Stalls, All Saints' Church, late 14th century.

ABOVE RIGHT: Gable cross from St Guthlac's Priory,
now in St Peter's Church.

BELOW RIGHT: Preaching cross of Blackfriars, 14th century.

46

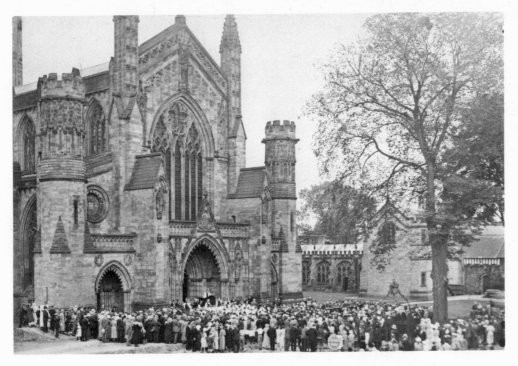

ABOVE : Cathedral west end and King Street, 1934.

BELOW : Cathedral west end, Silver Jubilee Service,
1935. Buildings removed.

ABOVE: Cathedral screen, 1864, Sir Gilbert Scott.
Removed in 1965.

BELOW LEFT: Old St Nicholas Church in
King Street, demolished 1841.

BELOW RIGHT: Wesleyan Chapel, Holmer Road.
Commemorative medal 1878.

ABOVE LEFT: Quakers' Meeting House, built 1822.

BELOW LEFT: Roman Catholic Church of St Francis Xavier, built 1838.

ABOVE RIGHT: Baptist Church, built 1880.

BELOW RIGHT: Eignbrook United Reformed Church, built 1873.

Merchants and Markets

The only Hereford craftsmen mentioned in Domesday (1086) are smiths and moneyers and there is a reference to women brewing—all in Saxon times but still continuing in 1086. There were by this time French burgesses, no doubt living and trading in the area known later as Frenchman's Street, now the eastern part of Bewell Street, close to the market place.

In 1121 the Bishop was granted a three-day fair at the feast of St Ethelbert in June, extended in 1161 to seven days. Henry I invited all his barons and burgesses to attend 'to have there as good customs as in any fair of England'. There was also a Jewish community by this time, probably in the present Maylord Street area, on the edge of the market. The fact that in 1189 the farm of the city was set at £40 gives some indication of its wealth; London, Lincoln, Winchester, York and Cambridge paid more, Bedford and Colchester the same.

Undoubtedly the castle was a source of wealth for it was an administrative centre, prison, garrison, military workshop and store and frequently a royal residence. In the *Liberate Rolls* a number of entries include that in 1241 ordering the sheriff of Hereford to pay £7 for the carriage of 60 tuns of wine from Monmouth to Hereford. In 1224 4,000 quarrels (arrows) were to be sent to Skenfrith and 7,000 to Chester in 1245. These and other references show Hereford as the arsenal for the Marches, while in 1227 four pounds of iron were sent to Hereford to bind the petraries and mangonels (military engines) which the king had ordered to be made there. In 1265 while Henry III was living at the castle for six weeks in May and June he carried on business as far afield as Devon and Cambridge, bought a horse for the queen for twenty marks, paid various bills for grain, 50s for 10 oxen and cows and £10 for the 'herbage of eighty acres of meadow'. Later, in 1289, John Warlegh and others were paid £45 10s for wheat, wine and honey they had supplied from Hereford for Drouelan Castle in Carmarthen.

From 1194 until the Jews were expelled from England in 1290 Hereford was one of their principal centres where Jewish bonds could be registered, Hereford having its own ark. This wealth must have helped the city and its trade. In 1232 Ursel, Leo, Moses and Abraham, sons of Homo of Hereford, a Jew, were ordered to pay 300 marks a year for twenty years to the king. A Jewish wedding feast of 1286 is mentioned elsewhere, but in 1287 all Jews were imprisoned and three years later banished.

As early as 1224 there were two mills in Yghene and there is constant reference in the medieval period to the 'scuttemulin' in the Eign area. In 1265 Henry de Dene paid the king seventy marks for the right to have a mill outside St Owen's Gate.

A good guide to the city's wealth are the occupations listed in the medieval cathedral muniments. It contains plumber, physician, mercer, stonemason, glover, miller, wheelwright, goldsmith, fisherman, painter, tailor, falconer, apothecary, dyer, baker, smith, spicer, taverner, porter, carpenter, shipward, mason, skinner, organ-keeper, corviser,

51

plasterer, draper, saddler, tanner, butcher, hosier, pattern-maker, woollen draper, and glasyer—sufficient variety for a busy medieval city.

There was an order in 1256 for a quay to be made at the castle, but as the king's wines were only being brought up river as far as Monmouth, it was presumably for purely local use.

Hereford's status as a cathedral town as well as a trading and administrative centre was undoubtedly a reason for its growth. The influx of pilgrims as the cult of St Ethelbert grew in the twelfth century, and even more after the death in 1282 and canonisation in 1320 of St Thomas Cantilupe, brought considerable wealth to the city. Even so the dual control brought its difficulties, especially as at the great fair of St Ethelbert, the citizens had to sell wool and hides under the same conditions as all other merchants, no matter whence they came.

The occasional record of irregular dealings is recorded, as when Ailmund was fined £100 in 1187 for using false measures of corn; the surprising thing is that he was wealthy enough to have paid off this debt in six years. In 1203 he is referred to as Ailmund the Rich. In 1355 Henry Cachepol and others were accused of defrauding Nicholas Negrehan, merchant of Venice; Hereford merchants were trading with the great commercial centre of the world. Henry counter-claimed that Nicholas owed him £500. In 1403 an inquisition was ordered 'of all who took or caused to be taken to Wales after the proclamation any grain, victuals or armour for the relief of the rebels'. Also 'timber, iron, lead and other property remaininge in Hereford castle after the building thereof and of the castle bridge were carried away'. It may have been good for trade, but it appears also to have been sharp practice.

Wines were still being brought up to the city from Chepstow in 1394. The wool and cloth trade seem to have been the most important in the city up to the Reformation. In 1354 the dean and canons had a water-mill and two fulling-mills and a little earlier there is mention of a mill at Luggbridge, but no indication as to its use. Saffron was being grown at Blackmarston on lands belonging to the nuns of Aconbury, presumably for dye for cloth. The industry received a severe setback when Henry VIII ordered the destruction of two corn and two fulling-mills belonging to the dean and chapter, perhaps because of their lack of support for the Reformation. In 1555 Thomas Kerry was pleading for their 'newe erecting and edifying'. This may have led to the molesting in 1565 of 'the fryse men and Welshe clothiers' who should have brought their cloth for sale at the Boothall, and perhaps to the bequest by Bishop Scorye in 1585 of stock to set the poor at work.

However, other industries were flourishing. Some idea of these is given in the list of twenty-two crafts taking part in the annual Corpus Christi procession in 1503 and the part they played. In addition to crafts already mentioned these included barbers, cappers, carders, chandlers, fletchers, mercers, vintners, walkers and a bellman.

In 1554 the blacksmiths protested that the goldsmiths, pewterers, cutlers, plumbers, braziers, cardmakers and glaziers whom they had admitted into their gild were taking it over with the result that a year later these other crafts were granted a separate charter of incorporation. Evidence of coal, ('sea-coal', as opposed to charcoal,) reaching Hereford is shown in 1558 when the smiths and cutlers were granted the first opportunity to buy it as it arrived.

Hereford's prosperity was perhaps best shown by the new market hall built *c* 1602 with its fifteen second floor rooms for the gilds. On the other hand there was a tendency to monopoly. This had already been shown by clothmakers in 1565 and by saddlers who wanted to ban the admission of 'foreign saddlers', while in 1617 there was a petition against 'foreigners' coming in to set up malt-making and brewing.

The economy of the city is evidenced in the gilds' minute books. They had the right to fine traders from outside Hereford and the mercers exercised this at various times against men from Coventry, Derby, Kington, London and Worcester; merchants were willing to travel a long way to trade in the city. An increasing number of boys were being apprenticed as barbers and barber-surgeons, six and four respectively in the period 1630-40. It was becoming a respectable occupation. In 1695, Roger Williams, a bookseller, fell into debt and his stock was sold. He had 120 octavo books, 8 quarto and 42 folio, mainly English, history and theology. His debts were £40; his stock fetched £35 6s 7d.

Flax was brought into the city for dressing, sometimes causing fires, for in 1700 it was resolved that 'no flax or hemp shall . . . be dressed or dried within the walls of the city except in such places as shall be allowed'.

In 1701 two bargemen were admitted as freemen—presumably an indication of river traffic working from the city. Hops, forbidden in the making of ale in the seventeenth century, were popular enough by 1760 for the collection of tolls on their sale at the October fair—farmed out for £4 4s. Also by this date there was a carpet manufactory in the city, but Hereford's main importance was as a market town and it is not surprising that in 1788 a thousand head of cattle was bought and sold in the streets at the October fair. Price in 1796 names cider, hops, and bark as the main articles of commerce.

An unusual transaction, and probably one of the last of its type in England, took place in 1802 when a butcher sold his wife by auction for 24s. In another earlier case the wife fetched only 1s.

For a time in the early nineteenth century shipbuilding played a part in Hereford's economy. At least eight vessels of 'large dimensions' were launched from Easton's yard opposite Castle Green between 1822 and 1832, varying from 200 to 80 tons. There was also a steamboat, the *Paul Pry* of 64 tons, launched in 1827, while another, the *Water Witch* was launched in 1834 from a yard above the Wye Bridge. This, like several others, was built for sale in Liverpool. Herefordshire oak was clearly making good ships.

By this time banks were becoming well established, having replaced the counting-houses in the inns. Perhaps the oldest was Hoskins and Morgan, founded in St Peter's Street in 1775. It was soon followed by Matthews, Phillips and Bleech Lye, (later the City and County), in High Town and the Savings Bank in St John's Street which was founded in 1816. The National Provincial was in Commercial Street by 1840.

The first book to be printed in the city was *Pascha* in 1721 and apart from a few breaks in the eighteenth century there has been a continuous run of printers in the city ever since.

Captain Radford, who built the *Water Witch*, also established a foundry in 1834 in Friar Street, but it was not a success and was later converted into a flour mill. Two smaller foundries continued for some time.

The more usual Hereford occupations continued; Benbow's glove manufactory was by the river below the modern St Nicholas' Church, flannel was made in King Street, there was a tanyard in Widemarsh Street, while the 1831 census records fifty-six cabinet makers, some of their more fashionable timbers being brought up the Wye to Hereford. Brick and tile making were flourishing within the city boundaries and still continue today.

As always, Hereford's prosperity rested on the county and area it served and the coming of the railways from 1854 onwards helped to increase its importance as an agricultural centre, the Bath and West Show being held in the city in 1865 and again in 1875. As late as

1939 a directory shows nine corn merchants, five cider makers, two mills, a hop warehouse and a wool merchant, while the heavier side of industry is represented only by the railway wagon repair depot and one constructional engineer.

Through the ages the city's prosperity has been reflected in its markets, centred for a long time around the great hall in High Town, and the fairs throughout the year—stock and sheep in February and Easter week, St Ethelbert's fair in May for stock and hiring, wool in July, cattle, sheep, hops, butter and cheese in October in Broad Street, stock in December and horses every month in Union Street. The sites may have moved but Hereford's prosperity still rests on them.

Millstones, Watkins' Imperial Mills, c 1920.

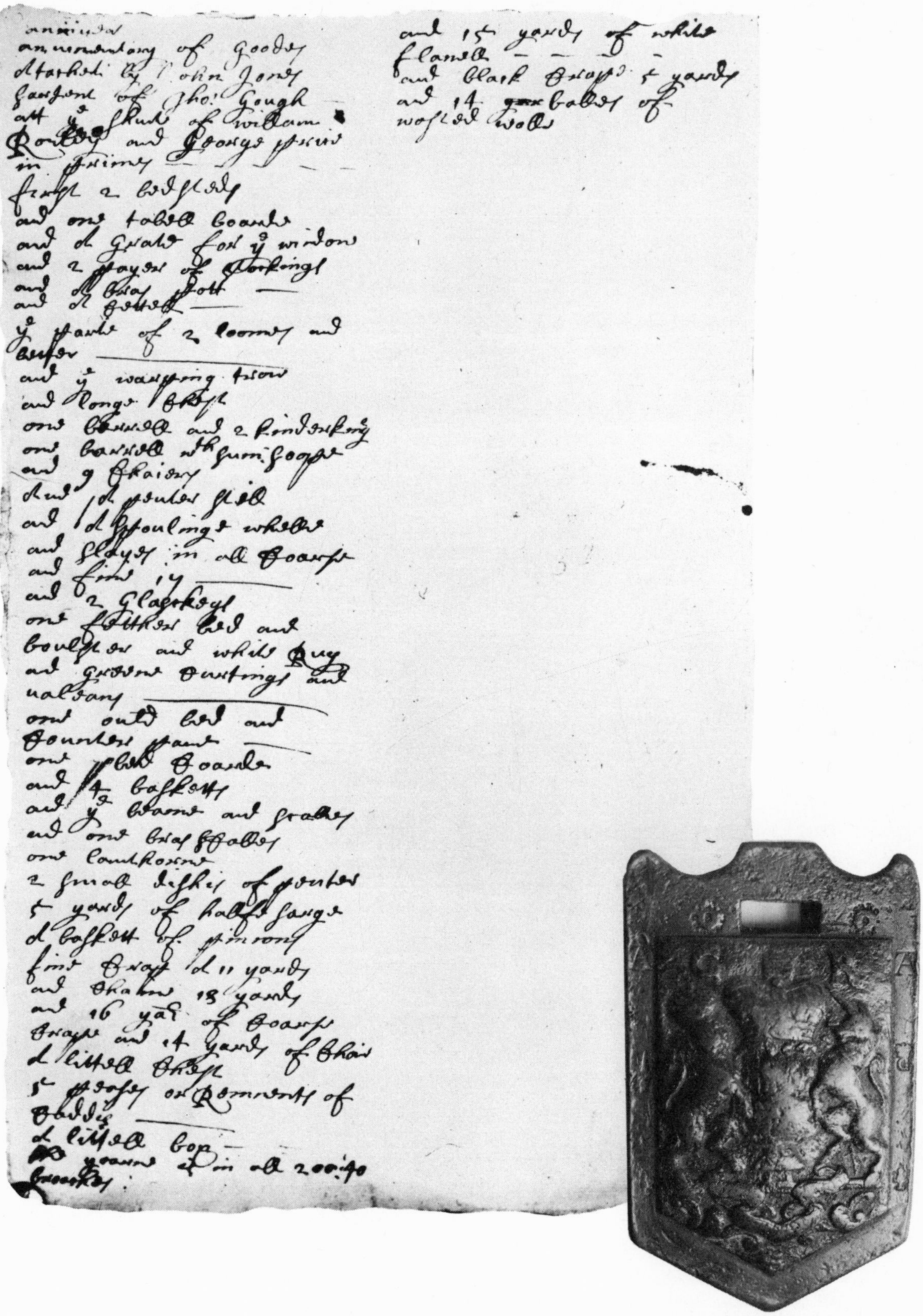

an inventory
an inventory of goodes
Aprased by John Jones
sarvent of Tho: Gough
att the hus of William
Rowley and George price
in Priney —

first 2 beddes
and one tabell board
and a grate for the window
and 2 payer of stockings
and a ... pott
and a kettell ——
the ... of 2 loomes and
gesser ————
and the warping trow
and longe beme
one ... and 2 ...
one barrell wth hum hoope
and 9 chaires
and 18 pewter plat
and 1 spoulinge wheele
and slayes in all coarse
and fine 14 ——
and 2 ...
one fether bed and
boulster and white ...
and green curtings and
valians ————
one ould bed and
boulster ... ——
one ... board
and 4 basketts
and the ... and ...
and one bras ...
one ...
2 small dishes of pewter
5 yards of half sarge
a basett of pinions
fine bras 11 yards
and shalow 13 yards
and 16 yar of coarse
bras and 14 yards of shalow
a littell bras
5 ... or remnents of
baddes ————
a littell box ——
sume ... in all 200:40
goodses

and 15 yards of white
flanell — — —
and black ... 5 yards
and 14 ... balles of
wosted wooll

Inventory of goods of Thomas Gough, weaver, 1679.
INSET: Wool Weight, ¼ tod.

55

ABOVE LEFT: Herefo

CENTRE LEFT: Th

ABOVE CENTR

BELOW CENT

BELOW LEFT: The

ABOVE RIGHT

BELOW RIGHT: Tit

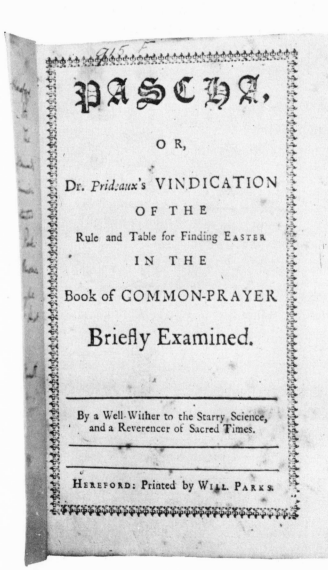

...s Offices. Built as flour mill, 1848.

...the boathouse, Vineyard Croft.

...Press. (H. P. Bulmer Ltd.)

...Mill (H. P. Bulmer Ltd.)

...Witch, 1834. (Hereford Museum)

...d Iron Foundry, built 1834.

...perial Mills.

...f first book printed in city, 1721.

PASCHA,

OR,

Dr. *Prideaux*'s VINDICATION

OF THE

Rule and Table for Finding EASTER

IN THE

Book of COMMON-PRAYER

Briefly Examined.

By a Well-Wither to the Starry Science,
and a Reverencer of Sacred Times.

HEREFORD: Printed by WILL. PARKS.

Here lie Interred,

The mortal Remains

Of

GAMALIEL DAVIES,

PRINTER,

Who,

Like an old, worn-out *Letter,*

(*Batter'd* by frequent use,)

Reposes in the Grave,

But not without a hope

That, at some future time,

He might be *re-cast* in the *mould* of Righteousness,

And safely *locked up*

In the blissful *Chace* of Immortality.

He

Was *distributed* from the *board* of Life,

On the 13th Day of April, 1803,

Aged 52,

Regretted by his Employer,

And

Deeply lamented by his fellow Artists.*

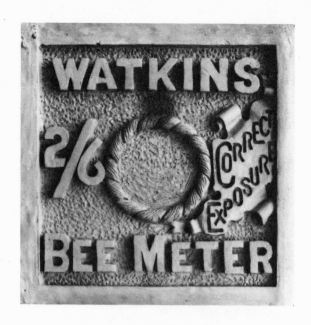

ABOVE LEFT: Tomb inscription to a printer, 1803.
ABOVE RIGHT: Advertisement for Watkins' Bee Meter.
BELOW: Bank of Hereford note.

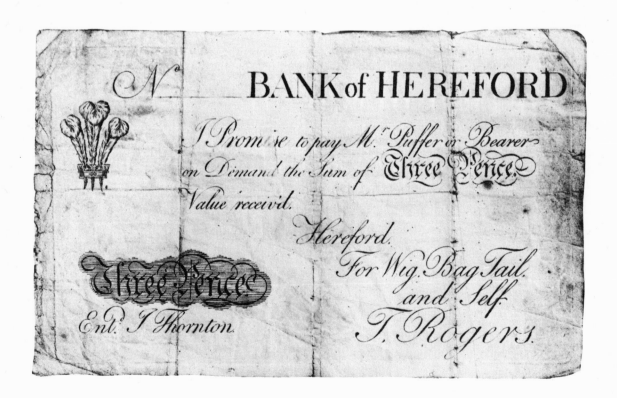

ABOVE: Corn Exchange, Broad Street, 1858,
W. Startin. (Hereford Library)

BELOW: Butter Market in High Town, 1860,
John Clayton. (Hereford Library)

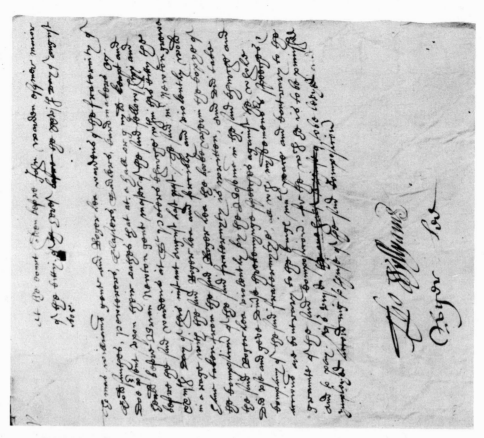

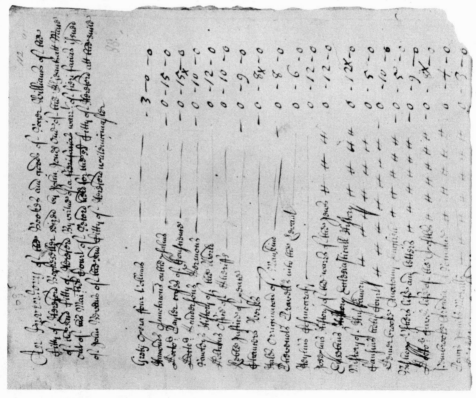

RIGHT: Goldsmith's complaint, 1605.

LEFT: Inventory of sale of books of bankrupt bookseller, 1695.

ABOVE: Butter Stalls in High Town, *c* 1800, J. Varley.
BELOW: Rope Stall.

ABOVE LEFT: Shop in Eign Street.

ABOVE RIGHT: Shop in Commercial Street.

BELOW: Interior of shop in High Town.

Gateway to Wales

Hereford's importance as a gateway to Wales arises from its position commanding the crossing of the Wye. Every English king up to the time of Henry VIII knew the city and its river crossing.

The Roman roads made Kenchester their centre; there may have been a ford on the site of the modern city then. Two fords, one by the site of the later Bishop's Palace and one by the castle site, must have been used by the Saxons.

The first bridge was built perhaps as far back as *c* 800. Certainly, Bishop de Capella gave help towards building a stone bridge soon after 1100, replacing an earlier wooden one. Exactly how it was built is not known. Probably stone piers supported a timber roadway, for in 1383 Richard II granted thirty oaks from the King's forest of la Haye and also forty perches of stone for the repair of the bridge. In 1941 it was under repair and the early piers went well above the spandrels, supporting this theory. The present bridge was built in 1490 and widened in 1826. Until 1782 it had a defended gateway at its southern end just like that still surviving at Monmouth.

The oldest surviving record of a quay dates from 1256 when the king ordered a wall and quay to be made between the wall of Hereford Castle and the 'water of Waye'. With its liability to floods and its comparatively fast flow the Wye has never been an easily navigable river. Various attempts were made to free it from weirs and mills, one as early as 1527, and again in 1661 and 1695. It was thought that these would help navigation, but after most of them had disappeared in 1727 another Act empowered the building of mills and weirs for better effecting navigation above Ross. From a scheme drawn up in 1763 it seems that 'trows' came up to Brockweir and transhipped their cargo to barges. An advertisement for 1789 in the *Hereford Journal* offered a barge of 17 tons for sale and in 1795 at Pearce's Wharf (near Hereford Bridge) the barge *Valiant*, (28 tons), and others down to 12 tons. As late as 1834 a steamship was launched in Hereford. Barges were pulled by up to six men or by one or two horses. From Hereford the smaller ones could get up to Hay and to just below Leominster on the Lugg. There were wharves on the north bank (Castle Wharf), on the south bank next to the Saracen's Head (Coal Wharf), and opposite Gwynne Street (North Wharf). In spite of this Hereford was still to some extent impoverished through lack of transport facilities at the end of the eighteenth century.

As late as 1857 the *Hereford Times* carried an advertisement of a new barge for sale and four years earlier Mr Wegg-Prosser had taken delivery at Hereford of a paddle-steamer for pleasure purposes on the Wye. A number of ferries have plied at various times, one of the last being the *Princess Mary* at Hunderton.

As early as 1774 there had been suggestions for a Hereford-Ledbury-Gloucester Canal, but work was not actually started until 1796. The Gloucester-Ledbury section was opened in 1798 but it was not until 1845 that the canal reached Hereford, the last main line canal to be completed in Britain outside the Birmingham area. Within six months there were proposals for it to be taken over by a railway company. However, as late as 1868, 28,000 tons of goods were carried, having declined from a peak ten years earlier of about 48,000 tons, and the canal continued until 1882. The wharves and basin at Barr's Court became part of the railway station. One major engineering feat in constructing the canal had been the Aylestone Hill tunnel, and it is a little sad to read of two donkeys falling into the canal while pulling a fly-boat through it in 1871.

Thus ended the use of the river and canal for trading purposes though the former is still popular for canoeing and rowing. It is likely that Hereford's roads, like those in most areas, deteriorated rather than improved until the eighteenth century. In 1729 came 'An Act for repairing the several roads leading into the city of Hereford' setting up a Turnpike Trust. By 1771 Paterson lists roads from London and Bath via Gloucester, Hay, Kington, Pembridge, Chester, Leicester and Montgomery.

Hereford seems to have had no stage-coach services until on April 28, 1774, Pruen's *Machine* started a twice weekly service to London, the fare being £1 5s. In September this became the Post coach and took one and a half days, the fare having been reduced to £1, inside, and 10s, outside. In 1775 came competition from Turner's *Hereford Machine*. By 1780 routes had been established to Worcester, Bristol and Shrewsbury as well as London with connections to other towns. The main coaching inns were the Green Dragon, the Redstreak Tree in High Town on the site of the present market hall, and the Swan and Falcon, where the City Arms now stands. On cold mornings it was the custom to fortify the passengers against the rigours of the journey with early purl, a mixture of hot milk and rum.

In addition to the stage coaches there were the slower, but cheaper, stage wagons which carried goods and some passengers. These ran to some extent as required, but there were certainly regular services to Worcester and Abergavenny.

By 1855 further stage-coach routes had opened to Chepstow, Aberystwyth, Tenby, Abergavenny and Weobley. At this date the *Bang-up* was doing the journey to Liverpool in fourteen hours and the *Royal William* to Kington in two and a half. The Nelson, Black Swan, City Arms, Mitre, now part of the National Westminster Bank in Broad Street, and the New Inn on the corner of Maylord and Widemarsh Streets were all in use as coaching inns, the stables behind the second of these still being intact today. The record time to London was fifteen hours, set up by the *Mazeppa* in 1837. Eventually these were replaced by the railways, but there was still a coach running to Hay in 1863.

Road passenger transport was not much affected by the tramway which ran from the Brecknock Canal to Hereford. The first two sections to Abergavenny and on to Monmouth Cap were completed by 1812, but it was not until September 21, 1829, that the third part was opened to Hereford. Its main function was to bring coal from South Wales and send Herefordshire produce back. Minerals, manure, apples and cider were carried at 1½d per ton per mile, and general merchandise at 3d. The tram house, counting house and associated buildings stood just south of the Wye Bridge and finally disappeared when the new road bridge was built in 1965. The tramway did not have a long life for in 1851 it was bought by the Newport, Abergavenny and Hereford Railway which opened from Pontypool to Barton Station in 1854, making Hereford the last English cathedral city to be connected to the rail system. This in turn was absorbed by the West Midland Railway in 1860 and this amalgamated with the Great Western in 1863.

Barr's Court Station had already been built in 1855 and eventually became the only passenger station in the city, the goods depot remaining open at Barton sidings until a few years ago. Lines were built to Shrewsbury, Worcester, Newport, Gloucester and Brecon, the last two being no longer in use.

With the coming of the railway the postal service was transferred to it and the stage coaches lost a valuable source of income. Hereford first had an official Post Office in 1682 when Mr Andrews was the postmaster at £36 a year. He would almost certainly have been an innkeeper and by 1733 the Sun Tavern on the south side of High Town was the Post Office. As early as 1639 Christopher Dawe is described as postmaster, and presumably his was the inn to and from which the carriers brought their goods, including the mail. They took about a week to London, arriving there on Fridays and departing on Saturdays. By the end of the eighteenth century the City Arms was the Post Office and in the early 1830s it moved to a separate small building in King Street, moving in 1851 to its present site in Broad Street. The charge before the penny post in 1840 was 6d per sheet for 15 miles, with higher rates for longer distances.

One of the first motor cars in the city was owned by Mr Parker, the city surveyor, and as early as 1900 the Smooth-Geared Auto-Car Syndicate were making cars in Commercial Road. It seems to have been a short-lived venture. It is interesting to note that Butcher, Marriott and Fryer, names associated with the motor trade in Hereford are first found in the market towns in the county. By September, 1908, there was a local motor-bus service run by Connelly from Barr's Court to Whitecross. This ended when the only vehicle was destroyed by fire in 1912. The first service to a place outside the city was started by Bird of Wigmore in 1919. The following year saw Fryer's service to St Weonards, Yeoman's from Canon Pyon, Bengry's of Kingsland, Pettifer's of Bromyard and BMMO (Midland Red).

In 1739 Willoughby Smith began *The Hereford Journal*, but it seems to have lasted only a short time and in 1770 was revived by Charles Pugh. It first cost 2½d, rose gradually to 7d by 1815, and eventually came down to 1d. It continued until 1925, then for a short time was not published, restarted as the *Hereford Observer* incorporating the *Hereford Journal* in 1926 and, after changing its title again was bought by the *Hereford Times* in 1932. The latter had been founded in 1832 and was printed in the city until 1966 when it became part of the Berrows organisation. There have been several other newspapers published in Hereford, but only the *Hereford Chronicle*, 1853-60, and the *Hereford Weekly Marvel*, 1869-1904, ran for any length of time. There was a *Hereford Evening News* for three months in 1882 and this is now being published again.

ABOVE: Grant of oaks and stone for Wye Bridge, 1383.

CENTRE: Wye Bridge, c 1830, J. Powell.

BELOW: Wye Bridge and 15 feet floods, August 1912.

66

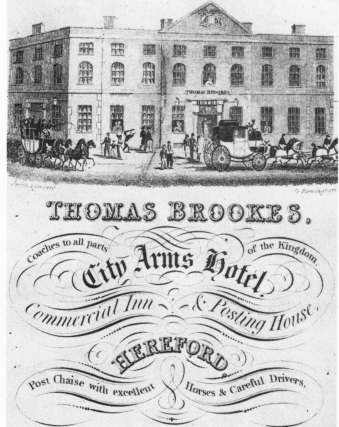

ABOVE: Victoria Bridge and Hospital, *c* 1900.

BELOW LEFT: Traditional Wye coracle.

BELOW RIGHT: City Arms Hotel advertisement.

ABOVE: St Owen's Turnpike, toll gate.

CENTRE: Aylestone Turnpike, toll gate.

BELOW: St Martin's Turnpike, toll gate.

68

ABOVE: Train arriving at Barton Street Station, 1860s.

CENTRE: Eign Railway Bridge.

BELOW: Wye Railway Bridge.

69

VOL. I. NUMB. 12.

THE
HEREFORD JOURNAL,
With the HISTORY of the
WORLD;
GIVEN
GRATIS.

TUESDAY, September 11 1739.

Copy of *Hereford Journal*, 1739.

The City Fathers

Domesday Book tells us little about the actual government of Hereford in 1086, but it does make it clear that at that time, as before the conquest, the city was responsible to the sheriff and, a post-1066 innovation, strangers were subject to the customs of the Norman town of Breteuil. In fact it seems that already, only twenty years after the Norman invasion, these customs had been more or less generally adopted in Hereford, for Rhuddlan in North Wales claimed in Domesday the customs 'which are at Hereford and in Breteuil'.

By the reign of Henry I the city had its own representative, the reeve, but it was not until 1189, by a charter of Richard I that it discharged its own financial responsibilities to the crown, when it agreed to pay an annual render of £40. King John's charter of 1216 gave the right to have a gild merchant which enabled the town to have more control over its trade and markets. The chief official was granted the title of mayor in 1383.

The citizens tried to exact some share of their £40 from the inhabitants of the Bishop's fee, but in 1227 and again in 1272 the king's courts ruled against them. In 1285 the city bailiffs arrested people on the lands of the Bishop. Edward I instructed the sheriff to secure the city's submission on this point.

During this period the sheriff was carrying out the king's orders in building, repairing and stocking the castle, but the citizens collected the tolls at the city gates, repaired the bridge and fortified the walls. In 1270 twenty-four weeks' tolls at the five gates came to £4 18s 5d. The city's wards were named after these main gates and the tourns, general courts, were held by the mayor twice a year in each ward. Tourns were also held at four places outside the walls between Michaelmas and All Saints, and at four other places at the boundaries of the city's liberty between Easter and Whitsun.

During the medieval period the city's jurisdiction gradually increased, a major step being taken in 1399 when for £100 the mayor and citizens bought from Richard II complete control of the law courts in the city. All pleas were to be held before the mayor 'en la Gildehalle'. That there had been a place for courts and administration is shown sixty years earlier when John de Tettele broke into and robbed the tolsey (town hall) of Hereford and was pardoned 'in consideration of his having gone beyond the seas in the king's company'.

Three sets of regulations for the city have survived from the sixteenth century and from them, and the remaining records of that period a picture of local government can be drawn. Prices were controlled and consumers protected as to the quality of the goods they bought. In 1557 good white bread was to be sold at two loaves for a penny, in 1576 beer was a penny a quart, neither hops nor ashes were to be used in making it and no bull flesh was to be sold until it had been slaughtered with hounds. This is a reference to bull-baiting, for it was believed, apparently correctly, that the flesh of an animal that had been made to struggle, and thus circulate the blood before being killed, was better and less tough. Good tallow candles were 3d a pound in 1557. 'Parking' seems to have been difficult even four hundred years ago for there were regulations ordering that horses and nags were not to be left in the market-place and salters were not to bring their wains beyond the tolsey.

At this time the old system of the 'Lawdays' still continued. These were the twice-yearly meetings already mentioned which were responsible for the type of regulation referred to above and the control of the gilds and entry to them. The 'Lawdays' were to be attended by the 'discreetest sort of the city'. The business was carried out by three inquests, the first chosen from the common council, the second and third officially from within and without the wall, but by the sixteenth century they had become to a large extent hierarchical and citizens progressed from the third, through the second to the first. From 1520 the number of the 'elect', (councillors), was thirty-one, and vacancies were filled by co-option from among the freemen of the city, ie members of the gilds; once on the council a man remained on it for life. Again this was hierarchical, mayors and aldermen being chosen by seniority.

In 1597 Elizabeth I confirmed all the previous privileges granted to the city in a charter of incorporation; it was the culmination of over four hundred years of obtaining rights of self-government from the monarch.

During the sixteenth century the national religious struggles occasionally resulted in letters from the crown as in 1553 when the city was thanked, really for not supporting Lady Jane Grey, and in 1576 when the Privy Council instructed Hereford not to elect as mayor anyone who would not take the oath to the queen.

The city and national archives give us a picture of life in seventeenth-century Hereford. The old quarrel between church and city went on, for in 1607 the citizens thanked the bishop for 'the light of the gospel enjoyed gloriously and multiplied by his presence' but were still prepared to query his authority over St Ethelbert's fair.

The Ship Money appears not to have been queried at first for in 1635 £210 was paid, but in the following year only £150 was paid out of £185 demanded. Joyce Jeffries entered in her account book '1638 May I Paid . . . for the shipping money for this yeare £3'.

In 1637 there were complaints that the High Cross in the market-place was in decay and 'that the *barlingams* or common washing place is in decay in defaute'. Mary Hodges was presented in 1662 for bewitching cattle; in 1675 there were complaints about the dangerous state of three of the city gateways, and in 1683 the churchwardens of the parishes were ordered to provide staves with the King's and the city's arms for the constables.

For hundreds of years the fear of plague was never far from the minds of citizens. The first visitations in 1348-9 and 1361 seem to have hit Hereford badly. During the first the shrine of the recently canonised St Thomas de Cantilupe was carried round the city in efforts to keep off the plague, and during the second the White Cross was erected by Bishop Charleton, markets being held there instead of in the city. In 1566 a letter from the Council of the Marches says 'it hath pleased Almighty God to visit the inhabitants of the city of Hereford with the plague of pestilence', perhaps a rather unfortunate wording. It was back again in 1580, 1604 and 1609-10, and there was fear of the great outbreak of 1665 reaching the city, for the inhabitants were ordered to keep their pumps going for half-an-hour daily during the hot weather to keep the drains clean.

There were other dangers besides plague and falling masonry from the gates for in 1693, as in other years, a number of people were fined for having wooden 'fimbrills' which caught fire easily. These were wattle and daub fire-hoods which could be dangerous if not kept free from soot. The constables were in trouble for allowing idle vagabonds and sturdy beggars to wander about the streets, and the Catherine Wheel alehouse was suppressed because of a riot.

In the eighteenth century the 'tourn' continued with the jury or 'inquest' 'presenting' offenders. All male householders were supposed to attend, but there seems to have been considerable absenteeism. The 'tourn' dealt with breaches of the city byelaws and there are cases of straying animals, erection of miskins (dunghills) in the streets, making a pond illegally and similar misdeeds. There was also the mayor's court which did much of the work done by the county court of today in that it dealt mainly with cases of debt in the city, and thirdly there was the borough Quarter Sessions. This covered a wide variety of cases: assault, theft, market and tolls, fraud, licencing, poor law, repair of highways and bridges were all brought before it in much the way that they would come before a Petty Sessions today.

The Assizes were still being held in the market hall in High Town, but a new guildhall was built in 1811 at the junction of Maylord and Widemarsh Streets, on the site of the New Inn, with the aid of private subscription and it seems that all city functions were held there, as also the meetings of the Three Choirs. A new gaol in Commercial Street replaced the earlier county prison in 1796.

In 1697 William III granted a charter confirming all the rights held under James I, and added a two-day fair in February to the three-day Easter fair already granted in 1690. Both these specifically mention the right to hold courts of pie-powder for instant jurisdiction during the period of the fair.

Although in 1862 Hereford lost one of the finest timber-framed market halls in Europe— it was simply demolished—it is fortunate in still possessing some of the best of the buildings associated with its administration. In 1392 it received a licence from the king 'because they have no house . . . in which the sessions of the justices of assize or of peace, or the pleas of the City, can be held' to acquire a tenement called 'Bothehalle'. Although apparently not used for official purposes since the eighteenth century or earlier, the medieval building still stands, with its fine hammer-beam and arch-braced collar-beam roof. The tolsey built in 1490 was demolished in 1770, but the house used by the mayor in the early seventeenth century survives as 23 and 24 Church Street with a well-worked plaster ceiling bearing the city coat of arms. The offices from 1882 to 1904 were in the Mansion House, that fine building of 1697. After 1819, pressure on space was lightened for a time by the building of a Shire Hall designed by Smirke. This and the City Hall of 1904 still stand and are much in use.

The Paving, Licensing and Lighting Act of 1774 led to the city being lit by 150 oil lamps and certain streets were paved. In 1781 John Lea was paid 4½d a square yard for pitching Bye Street.

The great nineteenth century Hereford event, as for all boroughs, was the act of 1835. Of 1,110 freemen only 465 were living in the city at that time out of a population of about 11,000. Only four of the old council were returned when the new act took effect. They and their thirteen fellow councillors had much to do. The city was lit by gas in 1836, a new police force was started in the same year, and in 1849 came the Fire Brigade, after a life had been lost in a fire in Widemarsh Street.

The main progress came after the Hereford Improvement Act of 1854, as a result of which there was a new cattle market in 1856, a water works in the same year, sewage pipes were laid and in 1860 the butter market was opened in High Town. They also had their problems. The new sewage system fouled the river, but negotiations dragged on until 1890 before a sewage works was completed.

The problem of a cemetery took even longer to solve. It may be regarded as the last struggle between church and city. In 1808 the bishop commenced an action for trespass against the mayor for issuing a writ for Poor Rate at the Palace. However, this seems to have been settled and in 1838 the long dispute over St Ethelbert's Fair was ended when the bishop sold his rights to the city for 12½ bushels of best wheat annually. In 1856 he offered eight acres for a cemetery, but non-conformist fears that it would be church-controlled led to a refusal of the offer and the land was given to the different ecclesiastical parishes in 1858. It was not until 1909 that Hereford at last had a municipal cemetery.

In 1872 the city bought out the Gas Company and a new works was built eight years later. Electricity followed in 1899, the first generating station being built by the cattle market entrance in Widemarsh Street. By 1905 it was supplying power to an area of 2½ square miles.

In municipal housing as in many things the city fathers were mindful of the rates, for in 1930 they bought 200,000 bricks from the prison site for use in houses in Mortimer Road.

Hereford has been an administrative and judicial centre for thirteen hundred years and in spite of changes, this continues.

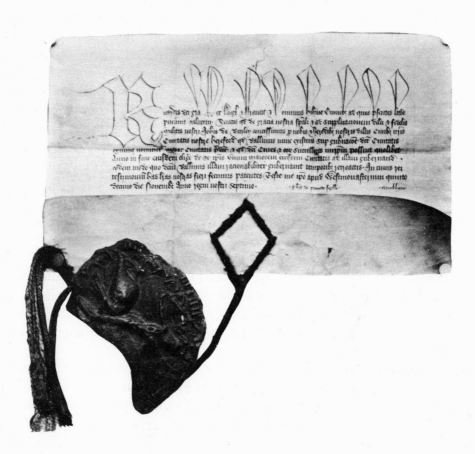

ABOVE: Hereford's first charter, Richard I, 1189.

BELOW: Grant of land by Henry III, 1265.

OPPOSITE: Charter granting title of mayor, Richard II, 1383.

75

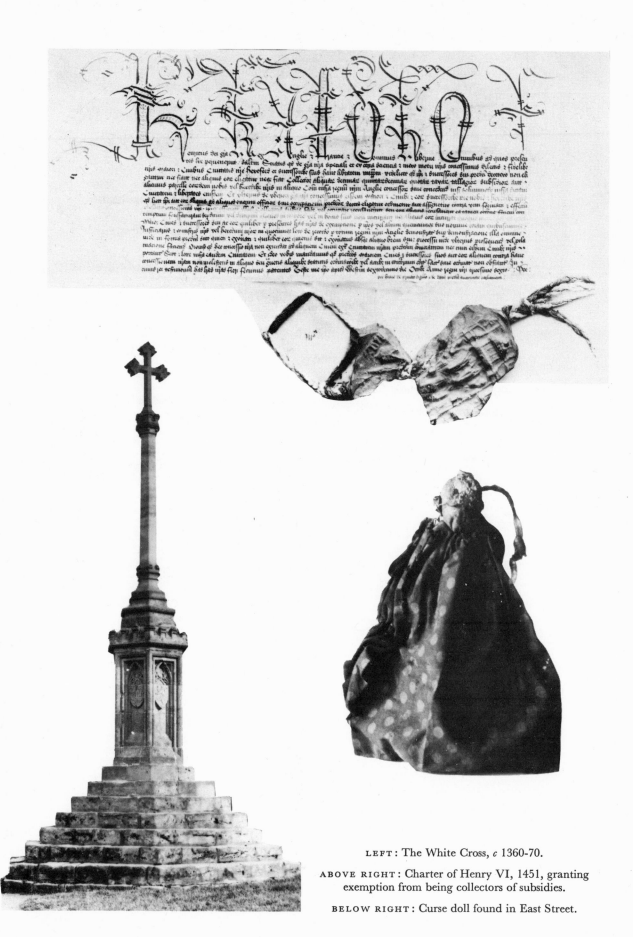

LEFT: The White Cross, _c_ 1360-70.

ABOVE RIGHT: Charter of Henry VI, 1451, granting exemption from being collectors of subsidies.

BELOW RIGHT: Curse doll found in East Street.

ABOVE: Charter of Queen Elizabeth I, 1597.

BELOW: Letter from Blanche Parry of Bacton, Maid of
Honour to Queen Elizabeth I.

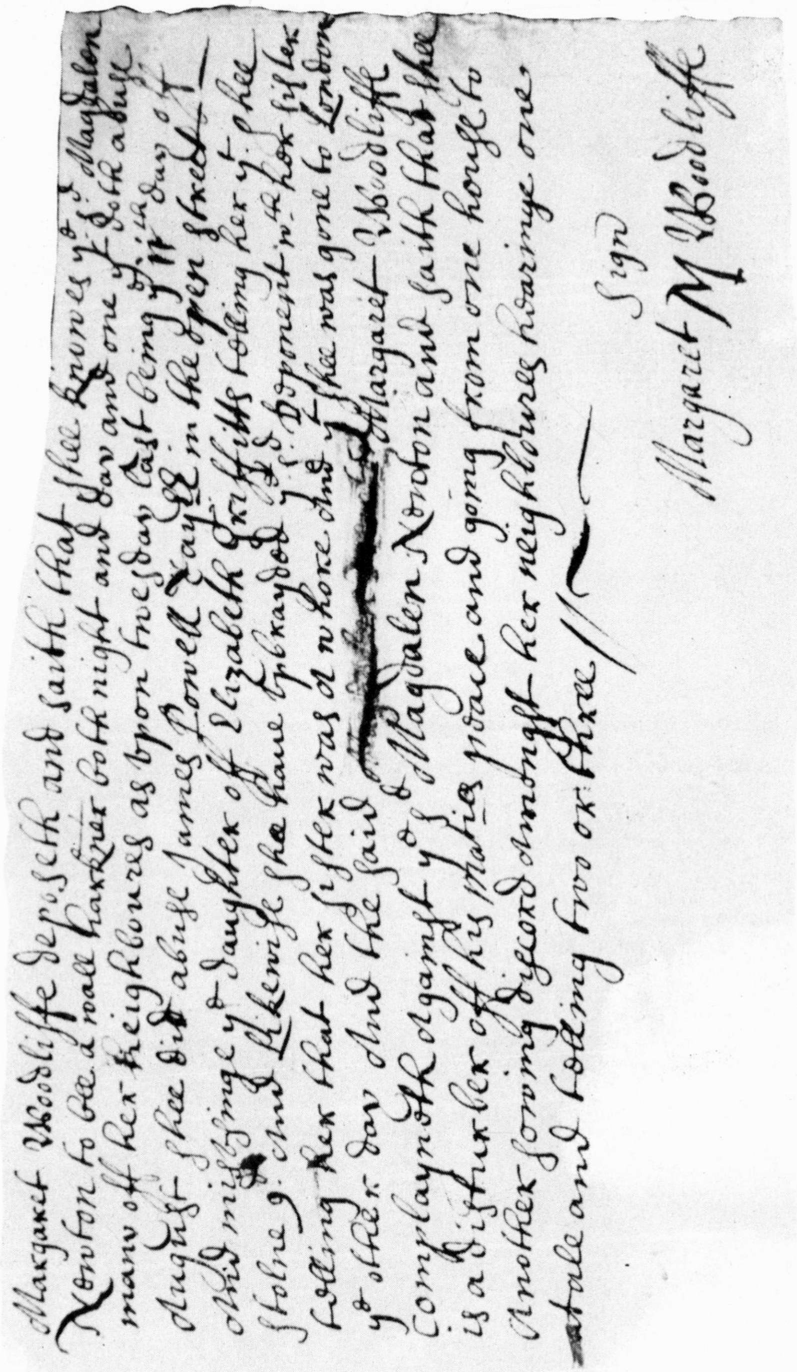

Margaret Woodliffe deposeth and saith that shee knowes ye sd Magdalen
Newton to bee a wall harkner both night and day and one yt doth abuse
many off her neighboures as upon tuesday last being ye 11th day off
August shee did abuse James Powell Tayl[r] in the open street
And misusinge ye daughter of Elizabeth Griffitts telling her yt shee
stolne [illegible] And likewise shee have upbrayded ye sd Deponent wth her sister
telling her that her sister was a whore And yt shee was gone to London
ye other day And the said [illegible] Margaret Woodliffe
complayneth against ye sd Magdalen Newton and saith that shee
is a disturber off his Maties peace and going from one house to
Another sowing discord Amongst her neighboures hearinge one
tale and telling two or three //
Sign
Margaret M Woodliffe

Complaint by Margaret Woodliffe against a gossip, 1661.

ABOVE: The Law Suit, carving in Old House.

BELOW: Petition wishing mayor 'external, internall and eternal happiness'.

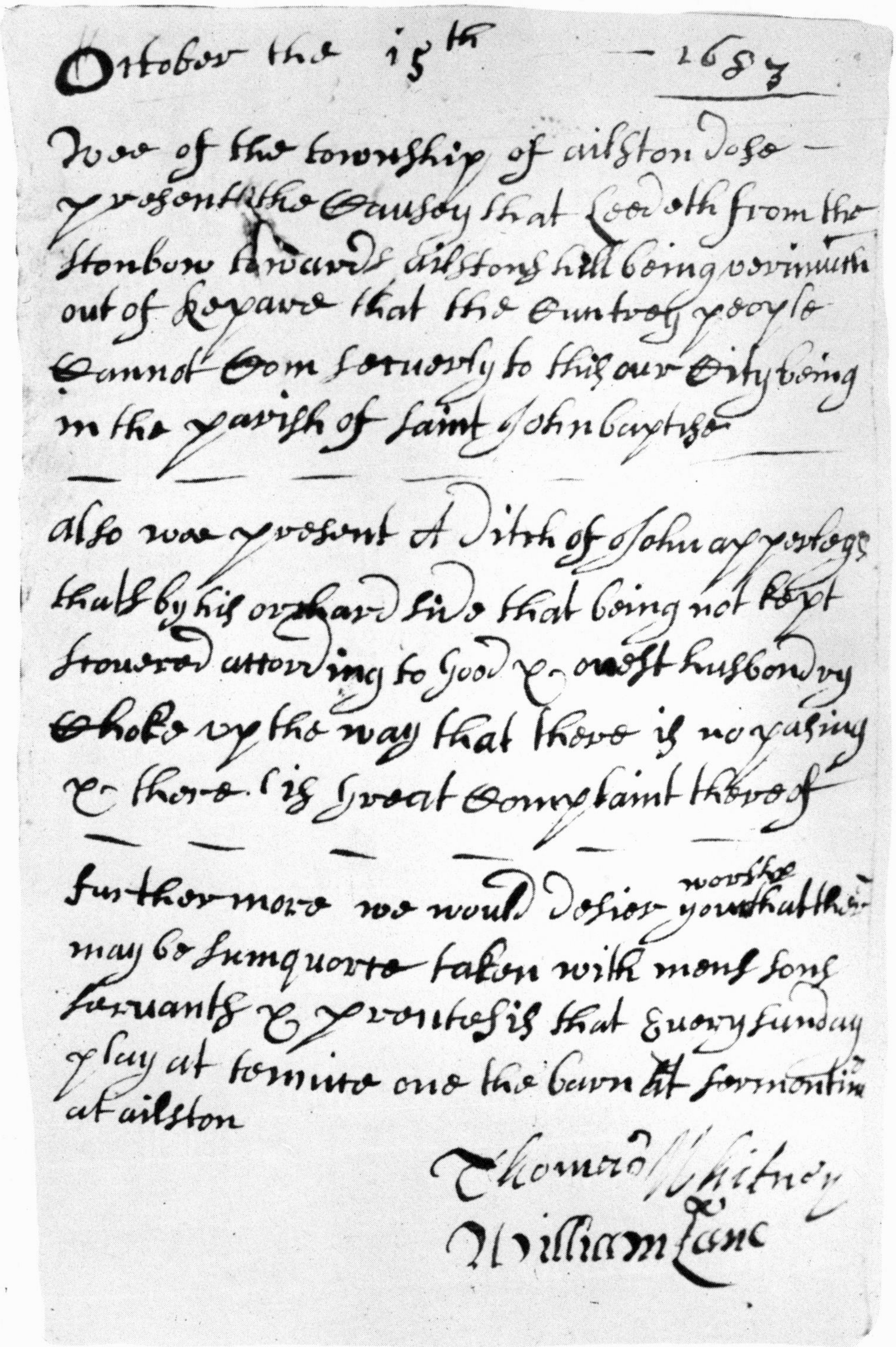

October the 15th — 1683

Wee of the township of ailston doe — present the Causey that leadeth from the Stonbow toward ailstons hill being verimuth out of Repaire that the Cuntrey poyle Cannot Com seruosly to this our City being in the parish of saint Johnbaytist

also wee present A Ditch of John as portege that by his orchard side that being not kept scowred attording to Good & onest husbondry Choke up the way that there is no pasing & there is great Complaint thereof

furthermore we would desier you that the worke may be sumquorte taken with mens sons seruants & prentesis that euery sunday play at temire one the bann at sermontin at ailston

Thomas Whitney
William Lane

Presentments about roads at Aylestone, 1683.

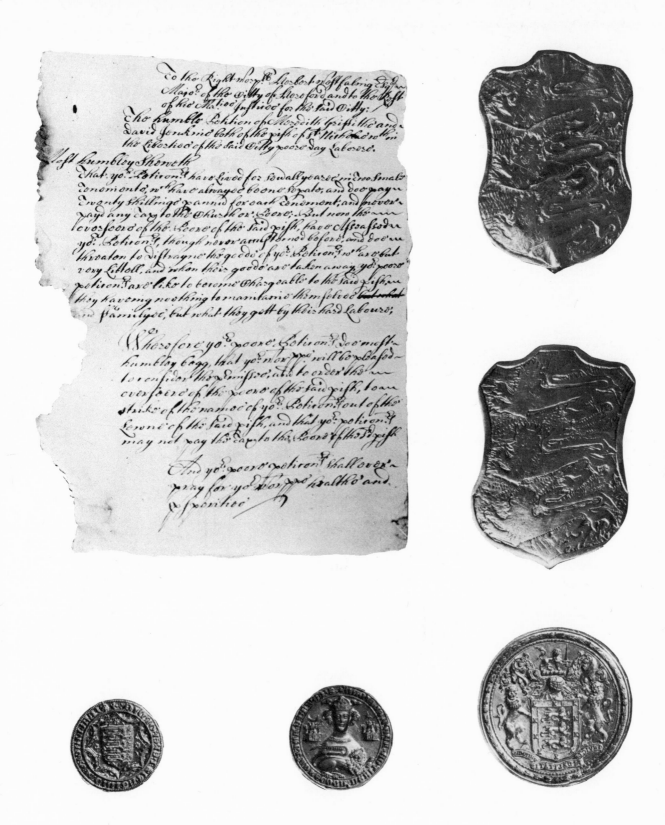

ABOVE LEFT: Petition for exemption from payment of Hearth Tax, 1683.

RIGHT and BELOW: City seals, 13th-17th century,
and arm badge, 1583. (Hereford City Council)

ABOVE: Charter of William and Mary, 1690, granting
three-day fair at Easter and Court of Pie Powder.

BELOW: Licence from Richard II to purchase Booth Hall site, 1392.

82

ABOVE: Fourteenth-fifteenth-century roof of Booth Hall.

BELOW: City coat of arms and plaster ceiling
24 Church Street, early 17th century.

ABOVE: Cook-house passage in Old Gaol, 1930, built 1796.

BELOW: The Shire Hall, painting by David Cox.
Built by Smirke, 1819.

ABOVE: The Town Hall, *c* 1602-1862.

BELOW: The Mansion House, Widemarsh Street,
from an old painting. Built 1697.

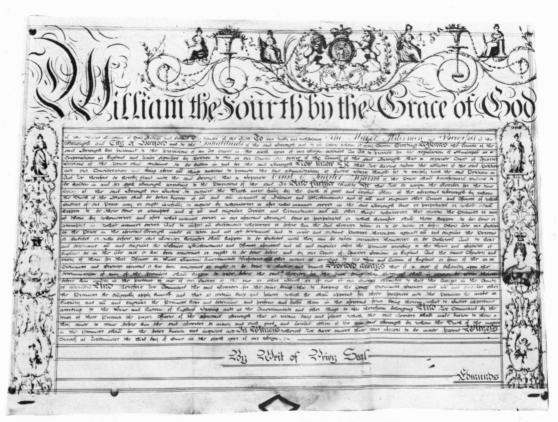

ABOVE: Charter of William IV, 1836.

BELOW: City's first steam fire engine, 1880.
Bought second-hand from Sandringham.

ABOVE LEFT: Civic procession outside library and museum, *c* 1915.

ABOVE RIGHT: Judge's coachman's livery.

BELOW: Judge leaving lodgings in High Town.

General Sir William Waller.

In Time of War

Astride the Wye and close to the Welsh border, Hereford has frequently seen strife. Down the centuries invading armies have attacked and occupied the city, and first certain evidence is the battle in 760, early in the reign of Offa, King of Mercia, when he fortified the city against the Welsh. (The tanged and barbed arrow-heads of the Bronze Age found in the Victoria Street excavations are more likely to indicate hunting than warfare.)

That there was fear of attack about a hundred and fifty years later is shown by the defences erected quite probably by Aethelfleda who defended the Mercian town 913-915 against the Danes. However, the enemy does not seem to have reached the city on that occasion, having been defeated somewhere to the south in Archenfield. Men from the city were sent to help defeat the Danes at this battle in 914.

The danger of attack must have continued, for the great earth ramparts were strengthened with stone walls. However, disaster came eventually, not from the Danes, but from the Welsh. Leofric resented the fact that Edward the Confessor had granted the earldom of Hereford to his Norman nephew, Ralph, and combined with Gruffydd ap Llywelyn to attack the county and city. On October 24, 1055, their armies invaded Hereford, destroyed Ralph's new Norman castle and burnt down the great cathedral recently built by Bishop Athelstan. Seven canons who attempted to defend the cathedral were killed at its door. The old, blind bishop died the following year and his warrior successor Leofgar attempted to drive the Welsh back from the areas close to Hereford, but was killed attacking Gruffydd after holding his see for only three months.

In 1088 Hereford was seized and occupied for a short time by the Norman barons in their revolt against William II.

The city next suffered at the hands of invaders in Stephen's reign, fifty years later. The king occupied the town and castle after a siege and recovered the castle from Talbot who had occupied it against him. Stephen wore his crown at a ceremony in the cathedral on Whitsunday, 1138, but his enemies did not give up easily, attacked again and burnt down all the city below the bridge over the Wye. Talbot and Miles of Gloucester fortified the cathedral close and even put engines on the cathedral tower to hurl missiles at the castle, which was defended by the king's men. These two lords, supporting the Empress Matilda took the castle, and after 1140 the wars of those troubled times moved away from Hereford.

The city suffered two sieges during the reign of Richard I, and was taken for the king in 1197 by Hubert Walter, the Justiciar.

Troubles with the Welsh were never far away and for a time in 1216 King John used Hereford as his headquarters against Llywelyn ap Iorwerth. Later in 1233-34 Henry III conducted his campaigns from the city against the Lords Marcher.

One of his advisers who spent much time abroad in the king's service was Peter de Aquablanca who became bishop in 1240, but was unpopular with the citizens of Hereford.

It was partly because of this that the city supported Simon de Montfort, the war between the king and his barons starting in Hereford in 1263 by an attack on the bishop in his own cathedral. Aquablanca was held prisoner at Eardisley Castle for a time. In 1265, on the eve of St Martin, Royalist supporters attacked the city, plundering the hamlets and villages outside the walls, but they were unable to take it even though next day they burnt down Bishop's Street, now Commercial Road, the area round it and 'the house of Aylmeston'. The walls, gates and castle stood fast. Simon brought Prince Edward to Hereford for safekeeping, but on May 28, 1265, Edward escaped while riding in the meadows outside the city. There are various stories of the escape but he seems to have been provided with a fast horse by the intrigues of Mortimer, and rode the twenty-two miles north to take refuge in Wigmore Castle.

Bishop Orleton and the Lords Marcher were among the leading opponents of Edward II, who seized the former's property in the city in 1322. In 1326 the Bishop's Palace was home for a month to Queen Isabella while she used Hereford as her headquarters against the king. Here his favourite, Hugh Despenser, was hung in High Town.

Hereford again became the headquarters of campaigns against the Welsh prince in the early stages of the war. In September, 1403, Henry himself came to Hereford and defeated the Welsh in battle, but not sufficiently to make them leave the county. For the next five years they were in and out of Herefordshire and young prince Henry, later Henry V, was in the city in 1404 and again in 1407, while his father was back for a time in 1405. It was these campaigns against the Welsh, using Hereford as base, that helped him to gain experience in war which was later to stand him in good stead in France, culminating in victory at Agincourt.

Queen Margaret and the Duke of Somerset brought Henry VI to the city in 1452 in an attempt to keep down disaffection on the Marches. Twice more in the next five years she was at Hereford with the court, but in February, 1461, the young Duke of York defeated Owen Tudor and the Lancastrians at Mortimer's Cross. Next day the defeated Welsh leader was executed at Hereford and for almost two hundred years the city was left in peace, neither national quarrels nor the Welsh much affecting its life.

What did have its effect on Hereford was the great Civil War, for here was a Royalist stronghold which became one of the key towns in the years 1642 to 1645. However, on September 30, 1642, the city was unprepared when the Earl of Stamford's army arrived outside Bysters Gate in the snow and occupied it for Parliament, without opposition. Stamford took up residence in the Bishop's Palace and stayed there until December 14, when he was called away, having no money, no credit, no bread, no provender, and the city was once more in Royalist hands. Except for a brief occupation by Waller in April, 1643, it stayed that way for three more years.

The great struggle came in 1645 when on July 30, 14,000 Scots under Lord Leven besieged the city. In spite of the destruction of the southern arch of the Wye Bridge, the burning of St Martin's and St Owen's churches and the suburbs outside the walls, the defenders led by Colonel Barnabas Scudamore held out for five weeks until the Scots decided to retire on the approach of the king's army. Charles himself dined at the Bishop's Palace on September 4 and, for their gallant defence of Hereford, granted the citizens the right to the motto 'Invictae fidelitatis praemium' on the coat of arms.

He also bestowed another honour—the title of one of his Majesty's carpenters, on John Abel, who had built mills under the castle during the siege.

Where the Scot's siege had failed, Colonel John Birch and 1,800 men succeeded by a stratagem. He hired six men and dressed them as labourers, who with a constable, were to enter the town on the pretext of having work to do. In the ruins of St Guthlac's, where the 'bus station is today, he hid 150 men with firelocks while he himself and a body of men lay in a hollow further up Aylestone Hill. At daybreak on the frosty morning of December 18, 1645, the constable and labourers went up to Bysters Gate when the drawbridge was let down, and while the guards were examining the warrant, first the firelocks and then the soldiers from Aylestone Hill overcame them, rushed inside, and took the city without bloodshed.

Life in the city as lived by a wealthy spinster, Mrs Joyce Jeffries, of Widemarsh Street, outside the gate, is given to us by her account book, which she started on St Mary Day, 1638. She had to pay ship money and contribute towards the training of local soldiers. It is interesting to note that John Traherne, shoemaker, collected the ship money. This is almost certainly the father of the poet Thomas who was born in the previous year. Later, in September, 1642, John Traherne goes for training with Richard Wigmore, his captain. Did he go to war as a soldier and get killed, and is this the reason that Thomas and his brother, Phillip, were brought up by Phillip Traherne, the mayor? In 1642 she was paying towards strengthening the defences of the city just before she fled from fear of the Parliamentary armies. The hardships caused by plundering soldiers are shown in her entries, her expenses towards billetted soldiers and even her help to a wounded man. She seems to have been quite happy to defraud the authorities and describes the man who helped her in this as 'an honest carpinder'. In 1645 the scorched earth policy in the suburbs meant that her house had to be destroyed. It had cost her £500 and she received only £71 5s for it. The hardships of war were felt by this old lady just as they must have been by the inhabitants as a whole not only in 1642 and 1645, but in all the previous attacks on the city.

Since 1645 Hereford has not known the horrors of a siege and only once the direct attack of war. This was early on the morning of July 27, 1942, when German bombers attacked the munitions factory and several people were killed.

However, its men and women have played their part in the defence of their country. In the regular army Colonel Viscount Charlement's Regiment was raised in Ireland in 1701 and from its inception wore the grass-green facings associated later with the county regiment which it became in 1782 as the 36th (Herefordshire) Regiment of Foot, the numbering having been adopted in 1751. It saw service in India against Tippu Sahib and was at Pondicherry in 1793. During the Napoleonic Wars it was in Minorca, Germany and almost continuously from 1808 to 1814 in the Peninsular War.

In 1873 the 36th were brigaded with the 29th (Worcestershire) Regiment of Foot and in 1881 became the 2nd Battalion the Worcestershire Regiment. Their first battle honour was won in South Africa, 1900-02, followed by sixteen in each of the two World Wars. On September 29, 1945, a proud city bestowed its freedom on the Regiment. In 1948 the two battalions united as the Worcestershire Regiment. A War Memorial to 2,000 who did not come home shows the sacrifice the county made in 1914-18 and 1939-45.

The Herefordshire Volunteers were raised for the last eight years of the Napoleonic War, and reformed in 1859 as the Herefordshire Rifle Volunteers. This became part of the new Territorial Army in 1908 as the 1st Battalion the Herefordshire Regiment. Since 1968 this has been represented by a company of Light Infantry Volunteers still based on the old barracks in Harold Street.

However, there is still a regular army barracks and unit in the city for since 1960, Bradbury Lines has been the home of the 22nd Special Air Services Regiment. The stranger would hardly expect Hereford to be the home of probably the toughest unit in the Army.

ABOVE LEFT: Letter from Colonel Lingen to Prince Rupert, 1644.

ABOVE RIGHT: Coatee of Hereford Militia, *c* 1800.

BELOW: Herefordshire Yeomanry Coat, 1803.

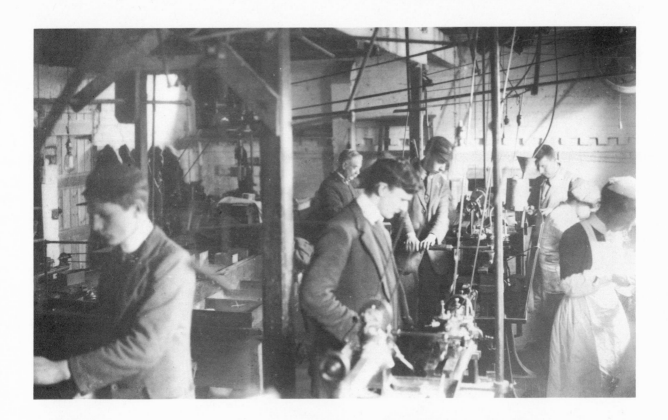

ABOVE: Munition Workers in Watkins' Bee Meter Works, 1915.

BELOW: Volunteer Fete, 1915, at Vineyard Croft.

ABOVE: Felling elms in Cathedral Close, February 1916.

BELOW: 2nd Battalion, Herefordshire Regiment,
Castle Green, April 1916.

94

ABOVE: Cenotaph in High Town, 1919,
made of wood and painted white.

BELOW LEFT: War Memorial, St Peter's Square, 1922.

BELOW RIGHT: Fire Watchers in Bridge Street next to Granary, 1942.

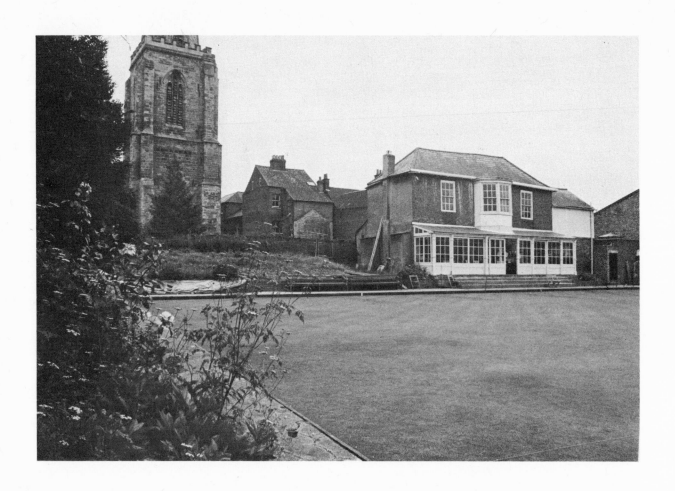

ABOVE: Bowling Green. (D. A. Whitehead)

BELOW: Pack Horse Inn; now site of Kerry Arms.

Hereford at Play

Today sport in Hereford is virtually synonymous with Hereford United. Since their famous cup run in 1971-72 the local Association Football Club founded in 1924 by the amalgamation of two older clubs has been elected to the Football League, and in the first season won promotion to the Third Division. Their black and white shirts have become known all over the country.

Organised sport in Hereford goes back much farther than this for there has been horse racing for nearly four hundred years. The races were being advertised as early as 1771 when the *Hereford Journal* first announced them on the same course as today, but in 1609 a famous meeting of veteran Morris dancers seems to have been organised, probably by Serjeant John Hoskins, and it is claimed that this took place at Hereford Races. In 1839 the construction of a grandstand was discussed, though whether it was built is not known. However, a new one was opened in 1965. The total ages of those twelve Morris dancers was 1,200 years — a list of names and ages still survives. Other entertainment helped to add to the fun of race-days as in 1819 when Tom Spring, later champion of all England (1823-24) gave an exhibition of boxing 'in all its branches'. Later he was landlord of the Booth Hall.

Cricket has perhaps not been the city's strong point for the Hereford club, founded in 1836, used to play XXII against an England XI in the 1860s, a custom which was revived by W. G. Grace in 1890.

One of the oldest bowling greens in England still exists in the city. It is claimed that it was laid in 1484 but there is no proof of this; the first specific mention of the Bowling Green, which lies behind the public house of that name in Bewell Street, is in 1697. In 1533 men were presented for 'boullynge' and in 1552 and 1557 'boules' occurs in the city presentments; so bowls was already being played in Hereford early in the sixteenth century and may well be on the same green as is used today.

In 1768 the city leased 'the Bouling Green and Billiard Room thereto belonging', but billiards is mentioned as early as 1662 when John Cole was presented for keeping a billiard table. By the mid-nineteenth century the Bowling Green Clubhouse was known as 'Albert's Billiard Rooms'.

Other games which had been frowned on by the authorities were cards, skittles and 'rooley pooley'. In 1655 Thomas Swayle was presented for keeping a 'disorderly ale-house where tippling and card playing went on during the Lord's day at the time of divine service'. In 1715 William Carpenter was in trouble for keeping 'an unlawful game commonly called skittles or a tenne pins' and for another unlawful game 'lately found out being called by the name of *Rooley Pooley*'. Was this really the modern game played by children on a grassy bank? Nine pins and shuffle board were also in disfavour. Perhaps these games kept people from practising with the bow and arrow, though it seems a little late for this to be the real concern; in 1632 'a paire of buts usuallie to bee kept in the Greene Lane have been carried away . . . and as yet not repaired'. More probably it was religious feeling that made these pastimes unpopular. Today skittles is again popular and since 1902 there has been a league trophy.

Hereford has always been plentifully supplied with licensed houses. In 1641 there were sixty-three inns and 154 ale-sellers; in 1825 the number was down to a total of fifty-six including the coaching inns. Only nineteen of these are still licensed today.

Other popular pastimes were the maypole, which stood in High Town until the end of the eighteenth century and, of course, St Ethelbert's Fair, now known as May Fair. The public whipping post and the stocks also provided their share of entertainment for those who cared to watch. In 1625 Richard Jauncey was presented 'for shotinge in a peece at piggons', an offence which occurs again over fifty years later.

Drama and music have played an important part in the life of the city. In medieval times there were the miracle and mystery plays, the great example being the Corpus Christi procession when the various gilds portrayed such scenes from the Scriptures as 'Noye ship; the good Lord ridyng on an ass; Joseth Abarmathia; Seynt Katerina with tres tormentors'. This continued until the mid-sixteenth century. The first permanent theatre may have been built in 1760, but there is no definite evidence until 1792. Certainly John Ward was producing plays in Hereford from 1761, Sarah Kemble (later Siddons) acted there as did her father, Roger Kemble. It seems probable that there was a theatre in Broad Street from 1760 and that it was rebuilt in 1792. On the other hand it may have been set up in one or more of the inns in that street. Not only plays, but musical entertainments were performed there, some of the well-known actors and musicians from London coming to play at Hereford. In 1856 the Grand English Opera Company was there for three weeks, but a year later the theatre was replaced by the Corn Exchange. However, it was an extension to this which converted it in 1911 into the Kemble Theatre which continued to be Hereford's main centre for drama until it was demolished in 1963. Three other theatres catered for Hereford's tastes during the period 1857-1911. The Alhambra Music Hall, built in the 1860s, was in Bridge Street, the Palladium in Berrington Street, (later the County and now the Regal) and the Garrick in Widemarsh Street. The diorama came to Hereford in the 1860s, the cinema in 1911 and the talkies in 1929; the Kemble had 3,100 people to see the first week of the films. The Alhambra seems to have had a short life. The change of name of the Palladium marked a change of function to a cinema, but the Garrick carried on until 1929, later becoming the County Library.

The Gilbert and Sullivan Society was founded in 1875, and like the Amateur Operatic Society and a number of other musical and dramatic societies still flourishes, while in recent years the Wiggins Pantomime has become an annual event in the county's entertainment calendar.

In 1716/17 Dr Thomas Bisse, chancellor of the cathedral and a great lover of church music organised a joint concert by the choirs of Gloucester, Hereford and Worcester cathedrals. Since then the Festival has gone on meeting in each cathedral in turn; in 1724 it was first held for charity and today this oldest festival in Europe is one of the great events in the national musical calendar.

Price, writing in 1796, extols the walks in and around Hereford, the 'very elegant public walk . . . called the Castle Green', and through the years the views of the river and activities on the river, boating parties, rowing and, more recently, canoeing have played their part in Hereford at play.

Another activity has played an important part in the life of the city—the Woolhope Naturalists' Field Club, which in spite of its name embraces all branches of learning which concern the county. It was founded in 1851 and flourishes today, having over 800 members, holding fifteen meetings a year, indoors and in the field, a week's meeting in another area of Great Britain and publishing an annual transactions. Before it was founded there had been since 1836 the Herefordshire Natural History, Philosophical, Antiquarian and Literary Society. A description of a meeting held at the Corn Exchange ends 'The company was entertained with coffee and calorie, cakes and chemistry, muffins and mechanics, strong tea and weak talk'.

The club was founded as a result of one of this society's meetings and takes its name from the Woolhope Dome, a Silurian feature of great interest to geologists. One of its members, James Rankin (later Sir James) in 1870 offered to build a museum for the club in the city; on being asked by the citizens to add a public library, he did so on the understanding that the Woolhope Club should have a permanent home in the building. This gift to Hereford continues today as the museum, art gallery and library in Broad Street and is still the home of the club.

The city also has the Old House in High Town which dates from 1621 and makes a natural home for furniture and other effects of the seventeenth century, and has in recent years acquired the Churchill Gardens Museum set in a garden with fine views over the city at the top of Aylestone Hill. The museum has a good collection of costume and a specially built art gallery used for occasional exhibitions, but also to house the works of Brian Hatton, a local artist killed in the First World War.

Libraries were not new to the city, for it has the two biggest chained libraries in the British Isles, that in the cathedral being the largest in the world, having 1,444 chained books. The total number of books is much larger. The other chained library is in All Saints Church. The 227 manuscript books in the cathedral library date from the eighth century onwards. The earliest printed book dates from 1473 and there are about seventy incunabula, (books printed before 1500.) The fine set of shelves and benches were modelled on those of Duke Humphrey's library, the oldest part of the Bodleian at Oxford. In the cathedral muniments, we find that in 1611 Richard Rogers, carpenter of Hereford, was employed to make these and in 1612 ten dozen long chains and eight dozen short chains for use in the library were sent down from Oxford at a cost of £3 10s, 4s for transport and 16d for the carriage of the money back to Oxford.

Today these activities still carry on and there is plenty of variety including archery, athletics, badminton, cycling, photography, rifle shooting, rugby, swimming, table tennis and tennis all going on within the city.

One last evidence of leisure activity is the recent archaeological discovery that there has been regular double-spit digging in Bewell House garden for some two hundred and fifty years.

ABOVE : Red Lion Inn, Eign Street.

BELOW : Gloucester Inn, Berrington Street, 1926. Demolished 1938.

ABOVE LEFT: Leaving the Three Choirs Festival, 1897.

ABOVE RIGHT: Garrick Theatre, Widemarsh Street, after fire April 1916.

BELOW: Rowing Club House, early 20th century.

Right playbill:

THEATRE, HEREFORD.

The Young Roscius.

Messrs. Hoy and Carey have the honour to inform the Ladies and Gentlemen of Hereford, that they have succeeded in making an Engagement with the YOUNG ROSCIUS (Master BETTY), who will perform on this and the following evenings...

On THURSDAY EVENING, AUGUST 20, 1807,
WILL BE PRESENTED, SHAKSPEARE'S TRAGEDY OF

HAMLET,
PRINCE OF DENMARK.
Hamlet, by the YOUNG ROSCIUS.

The Ghost of Hamlet's Father	Mr. M'GIBBON.
Polonius	Mr. WATKINSON.
Horatio	Mr. WHITWORTH.
Laertes	Mr. SHUTER.
Rosencrantz	Mr. RICHARDSON.
Guildenstern	Mr. ERNIMAN
Bernardo	Mr. RANDALL.
The King	Mr. CHAMBERS.
Grave Digger	Messrs. WATKINSON & SHUTER.
Ophelia	Mrs. RICHARDSON.
Player Queen	Mrs. WATKINSON.
The Queen	Mrs. CHAMBERS.

END OF THE PLAY,
A COMIC SONG, by Mr. E. SHUTER.
TO CONCLUDE WITH THE FARCE OF

All in Good Humour.

	Mr. WATKINSON.
	Mr. RICHARDSON.
	Mr. WHITWORTH
	Mr. RANDALL.
	Mr. E. SHUTER.
	Mrs. WATKINSON.
	Mrs. CHAMBERS.
	Mrs. M'GIBBON.

On Friday, THE EARL OF ESSEX; likewise, by the YOUNG ROSCIUS.—With the VILLAGE LAWYER.

Left playbill:

At the Theatre in Hereford,

On SATURDAY the 29th of DECEMBER, 1770,
Will be presented a Celebrated COMEDY, call'd

THE
RECRUITING OFFICER.

Capt. Plume, by Mr. DOWNING;
Capt. Brazen, by Mr. WEST;
Serjeant Kite, by Mr. CRUMP;
Bullock, by Mr. JONES;
Constable, by Mr. CARRICK;
Servant, by Mr. SMITH;
Justice Balance, Mr. BURTON;
First Recruit, by Mr. JONES; Second Recruit, by Mr. CARRICK;
And the Part of Worthy, by Mr. DRAPER
(Being his first Appearance upon any Stage);

Sylvia, by Miss KEMBLE;
Melinda, by Miss SHEPHERD,
Lucy, by Mrs. KEMBLE;
And Rose, by Miss BUTCHER.

SINGING between the ACTS by Mr. WEST and Mrs. CRUMP.

To which will be added a FARCE, called

The Honest Yorkshireman.

Sapscull (the Honest Yorkshireman), by Mr. JONES;
Elinder (his Man), by Mr. CARRICK;
Muckworm, by Mr. BURTON;
Slango, by Mr. SMITH;
And Gaylove (with Songs in Character), by Mr. WEST;
Combrush, by Mrs. KEMBLE;
And Arabella (with Songs in Character), by Miss KEMBLE.

PITT TWO SHILLINGS.—GALLERY ONE SHILLING.
TICKETS to be had at the Swan and Falcon, and of Mr. Woodcock, at the Coffee-House, in Milk-Lane:
Doors to be opened at Five, and to begin at Six o'Clock.

HEREFORD: Printed by C. PUGH.

LEFT: Playbill, 1770.

RIGHT: Playbill, 1807.

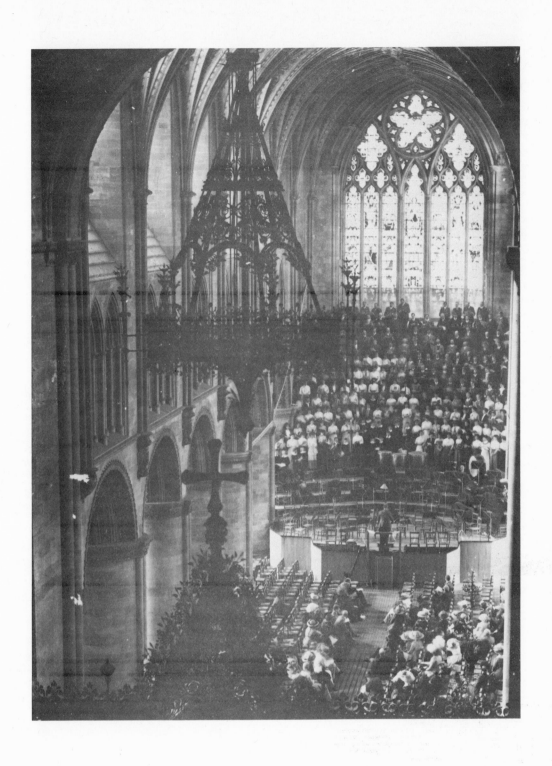

Three Choirs Festival, 1912.

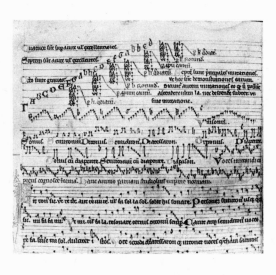

ABOVE LEFT: Seventh-eighth-

ABOVE RIGHT: Anglo
in Cathedral Libra

ABOVE CENTRE: Manuscript bo

BELOW CENTRE: Chained Libra

BELOW LEFT: He
c 1265 in C

BELOW RIGHT: Chain

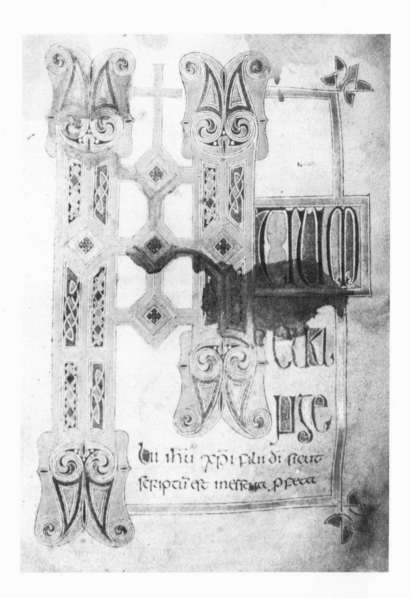

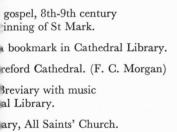

Uncials in Cathedral Library.

gospel, 8th-9th century
inning of St Mark.

bookmark in Cathedral Library.

reford Cathedral. (F. C. Morgan)

Breviary with music
al Library.

ary, All Saints' Church.

ABOVE: May Fair, High Town, 1893.
BELOW: May Fair, High Town, c 1895.

106

ABOVE : Paddling near Victoria Bridge, 1916.

CENTRE : Woolhope Club Meeting *c* 1860. (Hereford Library)

BELOW : Swimming Station, Bartonsham.

ABOVE: Lugg Meadows, Brian Hatton, 1887-1916. (Hereford Museum)

BELOW: Masters' Chess Tournament, 1885. Second and sixth in back row U.S.A. and Germany. Fourth in front row U.S.A. (Hereford Library)

ABOVE: May Fair, *c* 1910-20.

BELOW: Maypole, Queen Victoria's Diamond Jubilee, 1897.

ABOVE RIGHT: City of Hereford Motor Trophy.

ABOVE LEFT: Receipt from (Sir) Edward Elgar, 1886.

BELOW: Skating on the Wye, December 1892.

ABOVE: Small Car Trials, 1904.

BELOW: Hereford United A.F.C., beginning
1974-5 season. (Hereford United)

Civitas }
Exon ss }

The Informaçon of Nathaniel Williams of the Citty
aforesaid Scrivener taken upon oath the 9th day of
September Anno Regni Caroli scdi nunc Angl &c xxxiijo
Annoq Dni 1681. Before Abraham Seward Esqr one of
his Majties Iustices of the peace wthin the Citty aforesaid

This Inform{t} maketh oath that haueing a roome in the house
wherein mr Hann dwelleth in the Broadstreete wthin this Citty
to teach schollers to write, schollars belonging to Wm Hathway
Scriuener who liues in a backward parte of the said house
threw dirt at a table wth this Inform{t} did hang out at a
window of the roome wherein this Inform{t} did teach, vpon
wch this Inform{t} tooke the table downe and sent one of his
schollers to fetch it and bring it to mr Parrys house in the
Churchyard wherein this Inform{t} liueth, and some of the
said Hathways schollers fell on the boy sent by this Inform{t}
in Hathways house and tooke the table from him and
carried it to their master, who as this Inform{t} beleiuing
tore it, about two houres after this Inform{t} sent a maid
seruant of mr Parrys to demand it and mr Hathway sent
word this Inform{t} should not haue it except he came
himselfe for it, whereupon this Inform{t} went to one
mr Charles Hann to demand it, and in his the said mr
Hathways hall desired the table of him, vpon wch the
said mr Hathway strucke vp this Inform{t} heeles and did
fling him downe and gaue him one kick in the yard and
seuall others on his side, by wch this Inform{t} became
vnsensible, and was carried thence into mr Hanns
house where he lied for some tyme and thence was
carried home, and did spitt blood seuall tymes for
three dayes after;

Abr: Seward   Nathaniel Williams

Oldeschole and New

Whilst the Cathedral School must have existed in some form or other from early days the earliest known reference to a school in the city is in 1249 when the Hospital of St Austin was founded and consisted of 'a master, two priests, a schoolmaster and twelve poor brethren'. Little is known of this house and it was dissolved along with other alien religious establishments in 1414.

By 1365 an Oldescholestrete was being mentioned in various cathedral documents implying that a school had existed for some time in that area, probably the modern Harley Close. It continued to be called this until at least 1559. An edict of the Lateran Council in 1179 had directed that a school should be set up in every cathedral town; perhaps there was one in this street. Certainly in 1384 Bishop Gilbert refers to 'old custom', and a 'Grammar School' was either reorganised or refounded by him in that year when Richard de Cornwaille was appointed to govern the boys 'with birch and rod'. The lounge of the headmaster's house today is a fine open hall, 36 feet by 17 feet with main tie-beam trusses, arch-braced collar intermediate trusses, wind-braces with pierced cusping and brattishing on the wall-plates. There is a cellar beneath and the centre of its ceiling is strengthened to take an open hearth. It seems likely that this is the school of 1384.

In 1583 the money given in 1174 for simnel cakes for the canons was diverted to pay for increases in the salaries of the headmaster and usher. At the same time it was recommended that Mr May be appointed headmaster of the 'new free grammar school'. A new building seems to have been erected just outside the western walk of the cloisters and the move into this may well be the occasion on which the Harley Close hall went out of use. Clement Barksdale who was 'Master of the Free School' in 1641 became one of the clergy ejected during the Commonwealth. In 1665, rules and orders for the government of the grammar school were set forth by the Dean and Chapter. In 1796 the headmaster had 'about forty pounds per annum and a very good house'. By that date the school was in the Music Room, built on the site of the west walk of the cloisters, and so called because it was used for the Three Choirs Festival. Boys have always been boys, for in 1797 the chapter requested Mr Squire, the headmaster, to forbid pupils to play in the churchyard. The Music Room was built between 1762 and 1779. From 1835 the school was housed in the headmaster's house for a few years and from 1842 to 1875 in the north-east part of the College of the Vicars Choral. The present building on the corner of Castle and Quay Streets dates from 1875-76 with additions in 1881 and 1885. In 1911 the school spread across Castle Street and has gone on expanding, taking in the Old Deanery and other buildings.

In 1796 there is reference to girls' boarding schools, but the real growth of these small private schools seems to have been between 1814 and 1825. Fees ranged from fifteen to thirty guineas a year for full board, and one of the schools was actually in the Mitre Tavern. Clearly all were small and in private property.

113

At the same time charity schools were being founded, supported by the British and National Societies. By 1814 there was the Central Diocesan National School for boys in Eign Gate and there was a National for girls. These were followed during the century by: St Francis Xavier, 1835; St Peter's, 1837; St Owen's, 1838; St Nicholas, 1844; Lord Scudamore, 1852; Holmer, 1857; St Martin's, 1859; St Paul's, 1867; St John's, 1868; and All Saints', 1870. Of these St Nicholas and St John's have closed, but the others, with alterations and additions are still on their original sites, with the exception of St Francis Xavier. This moved quickly from St Owen's Street to Maylord, King and Broad Streets. Then in 1875 it settled in Berrington Street where it stayed for almost a century before moving to Venn's Lane. St Martin's appears to have existed for a time on the upper floor of a warehouse just below the bridge.

Long before this, in 1710 the Bluecoat School had been founded, and was from 1827 housed in a pleasant Georgian building in Blueschool Street, which was extended in 1888 and modernised in 1910. For a long time two schools, (one boys and one girls), in its later years it was for girls only. Its independence came to an end in 1972 when it merged with Bishop's School to become the Bishop of Hereford's Bluecoat School.

Lord Scudamore left money in the seventeenth century to found a woollen mill, one of his many attempts to help the county's farming and industry. Nothing came of this project and in 1852 the large sum which had accumulated was used to found the schools which are still named after him.

A school of a different nature was the Boys' Home and Industrial School which grew out of an incident in 1874 when two destitute boys were taken from the streets and given a home at a house in Workhouse Lane. By 1877 it had moved into newly-built premises in Bath Street where it continued until 1934 when it was closed by the Home Office on financial grounds. The buildings became the offices of the Herefordshire County Council.

During the nineteenth century the number of private, fee-paying schools grew. By 1859 there were fourteen boarding and seven day schools, mainly small and in private houses. Apart from the Cathedral School three stood out above the others: the Hereford Ladies College founded 1860, the Girls High School, 1865, and the Hereford County College (for boys), 1881. This last was in the building which later became the College of Education. In 1909 there were still seven day and four boarding private schools.

In 1939 there were thirteen elementary schools administered by the city as a result of the 1902 Act as well as the two high schools. These had been founded, one for boys and one for girls as a consequence of the 1902 Act in 1912 and 1915 respectively, though the first school to be built under the act was St Owen's Boys in 1903.

This act caused a certain amount of ill-feeling among non-conformists because they felt they were paying rates to help to support church schools and in 1903, 1904 and 1905 a few prominent dissenters had certain of their belongings sold to pay their education rate. They were bought by friends and given back to them.

As a result of the same act Hereford entered the field of further education. In 1904 the first local authority teachers' training college in the country was founded in the city. It still flourishes as the College of Education, having expanded greatly in its seventy years, though it now seems probable that it will have to close in 1978.

Further education was provided in the city as early as 1840 at the Mechanics Institute in the cathedral close. Later there was the Science and Art School on Castle Green where the Art College continued until its move to Folly Lane in 1969.

Since the Second World War other educational institutions have been set up; the Technical College of which the first part of the present buildings dates from 1954, the Art College, and the Sixth Form College, 1973, occupy with Aylestone School a fine twenty-acre site at the top of Aylestone Hill close to the College of Education. Thus all the further and higher education of the city is concentrated in one area where the various establishments and the Teachers' Centre can work closely together.

As early as 1808 a Mr Howldy was advertising a course of lectures on electricity; adult education therefore is no stranger to Hereford. It continues today in the form of the WEA, the University of Birmingham Extramural Department, the Open University, the evening classes at the Technical and Art Colleges and the Evening Institutes. The first two frequently work together and have been among the pioneers in introducing fieldwork and excavation as part of their tuition.

As a result of the 1944 Education Act there are seven additional primary and three new secondary schools in the city while the number of private schools in addition to the Cathedral School, has dropped to two. Hereford continues a long tradition of education.

Bluecoat School, established 1710; this building 1827.

115

ABOVE: Laying foundation stone St James' Infants School,
1896; enlarged from St Owen's.

BELOW: Boy's High (Secondary) School, 1912.

ABOVE: Teachers Training College, staff and
students, 1905. (Hereford College of Education)

BELOW: College of Education, founded 1904. (F. R. Boulton)

ABOVE : Herefordshire Technical College, 1975.

CENTRE : A modern Primary School, Hampton Dene, 1975.

BELOW : Herefordshire College of Art, 1975.

118

Self-help

Before modern local government, one way to helping one's fellow citizens was to found a charity. Many of these took the form of almshouses. St Giles', which seems to have been built in Norman times, and St John's, which may date from the late twelfth century are perhaps the earliest, but the first to be mentioned is St Ethelbert's, founded in 1225 by Canon Elyas de Bristol. No provision is made for its administration in the foundation, but under Charles I it was laid down that it should be for ten poor widows who were also to have bread and money. The tithe of the tolls or stall dues of St Denys Fair, October 9-11 were given to it by the city. St Anthony's followed in 1249 but was dissolved in 1414.

The great period for founding almshouses was after the dissolution, when the monasteries no longer existed to look after the poor. In Hereford there were Williams, 1601; Kerry's or Trinity, 1607; Shelley's or Lingen's, 1610; Coningsby's, 1614; Aubrey's, 1630; Weaver's, 1641; Price's, 1665; Traherne's, 1683; and Symond's, 1695. With the exception of St Anthony's, Trinity and Symond's they all continue today, whilst Traherne's has been incorporated with the Lazar House. Many have been rebuilt, some more than once. Perhaps the best known is Coningsby's in Widemarsh Street on the site of the hospital of St John's, which still has its earlier hall and chapel, and which is said to have inspired the red and black of the Chelsea Pensioners' from its own uniform. The most picturesque are Aubrey's in Berrington Street, a timber-framed row of buildings with the ovolo moulding and the short curved braces typical of the period just before the great Civil War.

These later almshouses were founded by gifts in wills, but the early ones were dependent on donations of money or land as a result of appeals by the church. Indulgences were promised in 1225 by the Bishop of St David's to those who contributed towards the building of St Ethelbert's, being followed by twelve other bishops over the next six years. A gift towards this appears to have been self-help in more than one sense.

These early establishments attempted to look after the sick as well as the aged infirm, one special case of this being the leper house which in 1272 lay 'outside the bar of Th yenestrete'.

Hereford had to wait until 1776 before it had a hospital in the modern sense of the word. Even so this was much earlier than the majority of comparable towns, being three years earlier than Birmingham and thirty-one years before the first hospital in Wales at Brecon in 1807. This hospital was at 42 Eign Street and remained in use until 1783 when the Hereford General Infirmary was opened. The money had been collected by voluntary subscription, the main organiser having been Rev Dr Thomas Talbot, who himself gave £500. Two new wings were added in 1834, increasing the number of beds from fifty-five to sixty, while in 1887 the Children's Ward was opened. The name was changed to County Hospital in 1900, and there was another addition in 1929. In 1940 a new County Hospital was built, and the Georgian block is now known again by its old name of General.

Some interesting facts about the early life of the hospital emerge from the minutes of the hospital committee. In 1794 the matron's salary was increased from £10 to £15 per year and in 1807 she was allowed three guineas a year for tea instead of two. However, not only tea was drunk, for in 1797 several patients 'were seized with a particular disorder . . . in consequence of . . . drinking beer . . . that was staler than usual'.

In the 1790s a lunatic asylum was built, apparently on the present site of St James' Church, and was in use by 1796, being administered at first by the governing body of the infirmary. It closed in 1853 when the new city and county asylum opened at Burghill.

The temporary hospital building was rented as a workhouse after the infirmary was built. Price in 1796 records that 'objects of distress' were 'very numerous' and that the different parishes agreed to establish a general workhouse. The problem of poverty became so severe that the churches and a number of leading citizens started a soup kitchen in a bakehouse in Packers Lane in 1829, which moved to Berrington Street the following winter, 'in Mrs Green's house'. The soup cost a penny a quart.

Perhaps it was appropriate that after the Poor Law Act of 1834, the new Workhouse should be built on the site of St Guthlac's Priory. As a result of this and municipal reform, most organised help was concentrated in the hands of the Boards of Guardians and the City Council. However, money was still needed, and given, for the hospital extensions; the almshouses continued their good work and there was the Rev John Venn.

This philanthropist was vicar of St Peter's, 1832-70, and was responsible for the founding of a dispensary in 1835 and St Peter's Literary Institution in the following year. The dispensary treated 17,000 people in its first twenty years. His great achievement was the Society for Aiding the Industrious, 1841. The flour mill built in Bath Street, 1848, belonged to it and in 1851 the waste steam from the mill engine was used for heating a public baths. The Society for Supplying Poor Women with Needle work, 1842, was another of his ventures and even in recent years almshouses have been built in Friars Street and additions made to those in Bath Street, as a result of charities founded by Venn. Hereford owes much to him and to Charles Anthony, founder and first editor of the *Hereford Times* who was responsible for the Improvement Act of 1854 and for many of the changes of the 1850s and 1860s.

Other almshouses founded in this period were Johnson's, 1863, and St Martin's Home, 1865. Even in the 1930s the Emma Cam, St Owen and Caroline Thomson almshouses were built.

Today in this age of the National Health Service and social security in all its forms, the Society for Aiding the Industrious still lives on in the city, along with many other charitable bodies, local and national.

ABOVE: Foundation of St Ethelbert's almshouses by
Canon Elyas of Bristol, 1225.

BELOW: Petition for relief by Richard Gittoes, 1659.

121

ABOVE: Coningsby's Hospital, founded 1614.

BELOW: Aubrey's Almshouses, 1975, founded 1630.

122

ABOVE: General Hospital, built 1783.

BELOW LEFT: Bread Shelf, All Saints' Church, 1683.

RIGHT: Price's Hospital, founded 1664.

ABOVE: Venn's Almshouses, Bath Street, 1940.

BELOW: Herefordshire Friendly Society Medal, 1838.

124

Thinker, Player, Soldier, Saint

Clearly some of Hereford's greatest characters are bound to have been connected with the church. Of these St Thomas de Cantilupe, 1218-82, Chancellor of England, and twice Chancellor of Oxford is the best known. Nicholas of Hereford in the thirteenth century was one of the first men to attempt to translate the Bible into English, while Hereford-born Miles Smith did much of the authorised version while a Canon of Hereford, 1587-1612. The Victorian philanthropist, John Venn, 1802-90, was also brought to Hereford by the church.

Also connected with the church was John Bull, cathedral organist, 1582-85, and reputed author of the National Anthem. Sir Edward Elgar lived in the city, 1904-11, and was involved with the Three Choirs Festival from 1878 to 1933.

Hereford has been the birthplace of one famous actress and two actors. The actress was Nell Gwyn, 1650-87, mistress of Charles II, whose grandson was later Bishop Beauclerk of Hereford. The actors were David Garrick, 1717-79, born at the Angel Inn in Maylord Street, and Roger Kemble, born in 1721. Kemble's children, especially Sarah (Siddons) became much more famous than their father.

Born in the city in 1565 was John Davies, poet and writer, best known for his comments on the poets and dramatists of his time. Far more important was Thomas Traherne, 1637-74, whose poetry was lost for over two hundred years, but who is now ranked with Vaughan, Donne and Herbert.

Artist Brian Hatton, 1887-1916, is mentioned elsewhere, but what is not generally known is that the master of works at one of the greatest English abbeys, Vale Royal in 1277, and later at Caernarvon Castle was Walter of Hereford. Another great Hereford craftsman was John Gildon, who between 1573 and 1585 carved some of the finest renaissance monuments in this and the surrounding counties.

Imprisoned in the Tower by James I, but later Serjeant at Law, John Hoskins lived in Widemarsh Street, 1601-22. Stringer Lawrence, 1697-1775, later General Lawrence, was baptised at All Saints. For twenty years he conducted the fighting in India and is known as 'father of the Indian army'.

The Bee Exposure Meter was invented by Alfred Watkins, 1855-1935, and was manufactured along with the pinhole camera in his works at Hereford. This pioneer photographer, miller and instrument maker late in his life propounded the Ley system.

The boxer Tom Spring, champion of England, is mentioned elsewhere, but in 1975, aged 46, died John Tarrant, world record holder for the 40 and 100 miles and one of the greatest ever long-distance runners.

In 1925 Hereford City appointed as its librarian F. C. Morgan. Fifty years later, now aged 97, he still lives in his adopted city. The city, the county and cathedral owe a great deal to this scholar, FSA, FLA, Hon MA of Birmingham, who still looks after the cathedral library, and in 1975 has been appointed Chief Steward of the City, Hereford's highest honour.

Nell Gwyn, 1650-87 by Peter Lely. (Mansell Collection)

Nell Gwyn's birthplace, Gwynne Street (Pipe Lane). Now demolished.

ABOVE LEFT: General Stringer Lawrence, 1697-1775.
(Mansell Collection)

ABOVE RIGHT: William Brewster, 1665-1715.

BELOW LEFT: Rev Dr Thomas Talbot, founder of
Hereford General Infirmary 1776.

BELOW RIGHT: James Wathen, 1751-1828, by A. J. Oliver.

LEFT: David Garrick, 1717-79 by Thomas
Gainsborough. (Mansell Collection)

ABOVE RIGHT: Roger Kemble, born 1721.

BELOW RIGHT: David Cox, 1783-1859 (drawing 1855).

ABOVE LEFT: Tom Spring, Champion of England, 1824.

BELOW LEFT: Edwin Ladmore, gunmaker, 1858, aged 41.

BELOW RIGHT: Walter Pilley, Mayor and donator of Pilley Collection to the City. (Photograph 1912)

ABOVE RIGHT: Alfred Watkins, 1855-1935.

The Fourteenth Century

After some thirteen hundred years Hereford today presents a picture its earlier inhabitants would not recognise. From 24,163 in 1931 its population had risen to 46,950 by 1971. Within it is the world's biggest cider manufacturer, H. P. Bulmer Ltd,. and Henry Wiggin and Co., the largest and most modern nickel alloy works in Europe. Agricultural-based industries continue—canning, poultry and egg production on a large scale and flour milling—as well as the long-standing tile manufacture. The city's industry has been diversified by valve production, steel fabricating and galvanising, specialised refrigeration equipment production, lighting, engine parts and printing, the last another long-standing Hereford industry. Unfortunately it no longer prints its own newspaper, nor has its own theatre, but it has a fine new cattle market and the gradual growth of tourism is bringing another new and important industry quietly into the city.

The last ten years have seen the coming of the ring road, the rise to fame of Hereford United, the excavation of some of the city's past and the exposure of much of its old wall. It has also seen the building of a Church of the Latter Day Saints, these enterprising missionaries viewing Hereford as a place in which they should work.

Now, in the last year has come local government reorganisation, removing from the city after this long period, some of its status as a county town, but leaving its municipal powers virtually unaltered, as confirmed by its latest charter granted by Queen Elizabeth II. Its mayor and council continue, and even if it has lost the Assizes, a Crown Court and a Petty Sessions are still held.

In other spheres it is threatened by the closure of its College of Education, the first local authority establishment of this type in the country.

There are plans for redevelopment inside the walls. What will happen is not yet known, but whatever it is, may it be thoughtfully and carefully planned so as not to harm, but to enhance this ancient city. Its story is one of change and no community can live without it, but behind the story is a strong, enduring thread of continuity, of strength and resilience. May Hereford continue in this fashion.

ABOVE LEFT: Opening of the 1975 May Fair. (The Hereford Times)

ABOVE RIGHT: Church Street, 1975, looking south.

BELOW: High Town, 1975. (The Hereford Times).

ABOVE LEFT: Eign Gate, 1975.

ABOVE RIGHT: Hereford Butter Market, before the pedestrian precinct. (The Hereford Times)

BELOW: Cattle Market, 1975.

ABOVE LEFT: Church Street, 1975, looking north.

ABOVE RIGHT: Ancient and modern: Greyfriars Bridge and Wye Bridge.
(The Hereford Times)

BELOW: King George V, Britain's most powerful locomotive,
now working for H. P. Bulmer Ltd. (The Hereford Times)

134

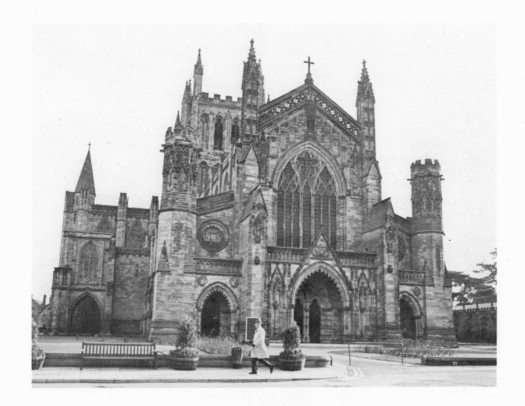

ABOVE LEFT: Apples arriving at H. P. Bulmer Ltd. (H. P. Bulmer Ltd)

ABOVE RIGHT: Cider vats at H. P. Bulmer Ltd. (H. P. Bulmer Ltd)

BELOW: Hereford Cathedral West front—as today's
visitors see it. (The Hereford Times)

'Urbs in rure', Henry Wiggin & Co Ltd Works.
(Henry Wiggin & Co Ltd)

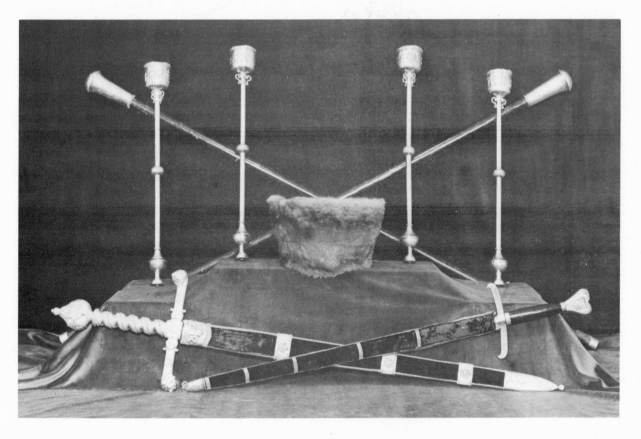

ABOVE: The Changing City: demolition of the old Fire
Station, October 1975. (The Hereford Times)

BELOW: Civic Tradition: City maces, staves, swords and
hat of maintenance. (Hereford City Council)

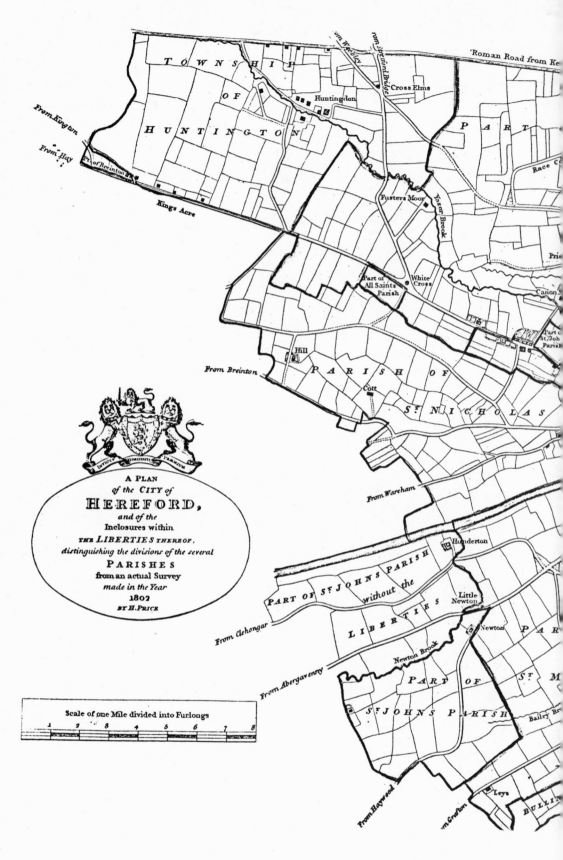

A PLAN
of the CITY of
HEREFORD,
and of the
Inclosures within
THE *LIBERTIES* THEREOF,
distinguishing the divisions of the several
PARISHES
from an actual Survey
made in the Year
1802
BY H. PRICE

Scale of one Mile divided into Furlongs

1   2   3   4   5   6   7   8

1802 map of Heref...
virtually uncha...

138

to Worcester
To Leominster
To Shelwick
Lug Bridge
Lug R.
Part of Lug Meadow
THE PARISH OF
OLMER
PARISH OF
ALL SAINTS
PART
OF THE
TOWNSHIP OF
TUPSLEY
Barrs Court
Aylston Hill
the Folly
To Lugwardine
Cock
Tupsley Green
Monkmoor Mill
St. Johns
Parish
Gaol
St. PETERS
PARISH
Scutt Mill
Tupsley
Friars
Castle Green
Castle Mill
Lunatic Asylum
Infirmary
Eign Mill
Eign
Vineyard
Litley
PARISH
OF
St. OWEN
Bartonsham
RIVER WYE
Franchise Stone
Hinton
Putson Stile
Putson
To Rotherwas
Cottage
Lower Bullingham
Withy Brook
To Ross
Brick Kiln
Red Hill
From Bullingham
The Castle Green not in the Liberties of the City
Pk. Turnpikes.

owing the liberties—still
(Hereford Library)

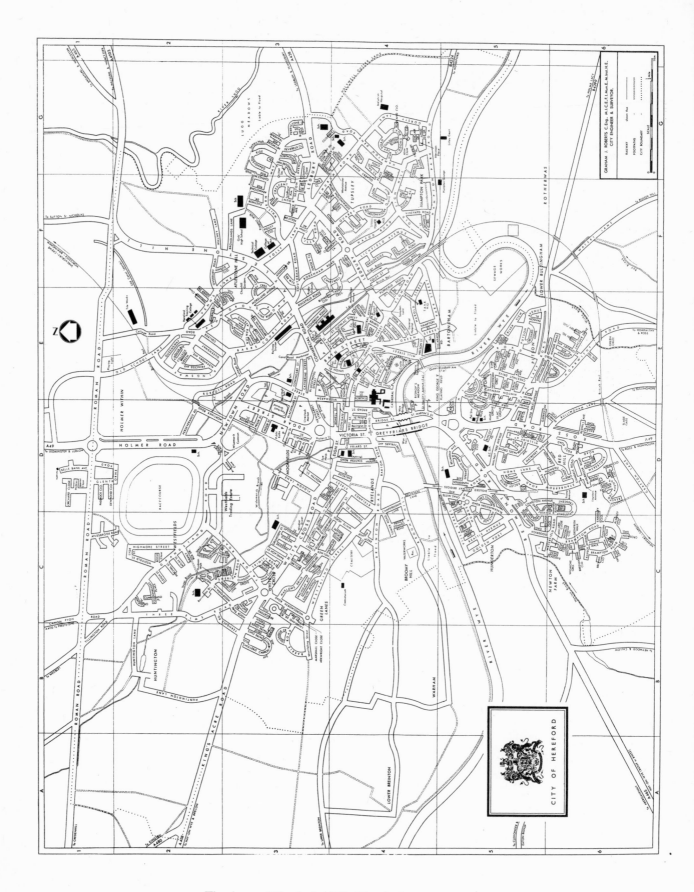

The shape of Hereford, 1973. (Hereford City Council)

CALENDAR FOR HEREFORD

c 600-500 BC	Bronze Age man leaves his weapons at Fayre Oaks
c 400	Iron Age settlers at Credenhill
c 75 AD	Romans at Kenchester stay about 300 years
c 500	Corn-drying ovens constructed near Victoria Street
669	Bishop Putta at Hereford
676	Bishopric founded
736-40	Cuthbert, Bishop of Hereford
760	Area attacked by Welsh. Offa probably built first rampart
Late 8 cent.	Original St Guthlac's founded
792	Murder of Ethelbert
c 800	Probable building of first bridge
914	Vikings defeated to south of city and new rampart probably built by Aethelfleda
930	Welsh princes pay tribute to Athelstan at Hereford
c 1030-40	New stone cathedral built
c 1050	Castle built
1055	City destroyed by Llywelyn and Aelfgar
c 1060	New stone defences built
c 1080	Building of new cathedral begun
1085	St Peter's Church founded
1086	Domesday Book
c 1100	Bridge built, probably with stone piers
1121	Grant of a three-day fair in June
c 1140	St Guthlac's moved to new site outside walls
c 1145	Cathedral consecrated
c 1180	Bishop's Palace built
1189	Richard I grants city's first charter
Early 13 cent.	All Saints' Church founded
c 1250	Grey Friars established in city
1256	First record of a quay
1265	Suburbs destroyed to prevent use by rebel barons
	Escape of Prince Edward (later Edward I) from castle
1278-82	Thomas Cantilupe Bishop
1290	Expulsion of Jews
c 1319	Black Friars established in Widemarsh Street
1320	Canonisation of St Thomas Cantilupe
1348-9	Plague first hits Hereford
c 1372-82	Nicholas de Hereford translating Bible
1382	Chief official granted title of Mayor
1384	Refounding of Cathedral School
1392	Boothhall site acquired
1399	Richard II grants corporation charge of its own lawcourts
1461	Battle of Mortimer's Cross. Owen Tudor executed at Hereford
1472-5	New College of Vicars Choral built
1490	Present Wye Bridge built
	Tolsey built in High Town
1536-9	Dissolution of religious houses
1587-1612	Miles Smith working on Authorised Version of Bible
1597	Queen Elizabeth I confirms all previous privileges
c 1602	New market hall built
1609-10	Plague in city for last time
1642	City occupied for Parliament, September to December
1645	Scots besiege city, July to September, but fail to take it
	December, Colonel Birch captures Hereford
	Keep of castle razed
1650	Nell Gwyn born in Pipe Lane (Gwynne Street)

1679	Execution of John Kemble
1682	First official Post Office in city
1690	Grant of three-day fair at Easter
1697	William III grants charter and two-day fair in February
1710	Bluecoat School founded
1716	Three Choirs Festival inaugurated
1721	Pascha. First book to be printed in the city
1739	Hereford Journal first published
1760	First theatre probably built
1770	Tolsey demolished
1774	Pruen's stage-coach service to London started
	Paving, Licensing and Lighting Act
1782-98	City gateways demolished
1783	Hereford General Infirmary opened
1786	Collapse of west end of cathedral
1796	New gaol built
	John Price's Hereford published
1811	Guildhall built in Widemarsh Street
1819	Shire Hall built by Smirke
1822	New Quakers' Meeting House built
1826	Wye Bridge widened
1829	Abergavenny-Hereford tramway completed
1832	First Reform Act
	Rev John Venn becomes Vicar of St Peter's
	Hereford Times founded by Charles Anthony
1835	Municipal Corporations Act
1836	City lit by gas
1838	City bought rights over St Ethelbert's Fair from Bishop
	St Francis Xavier Church built
1841	Society for Aiding the Industrious founded
1842	St Nicholas' Church built
1845	Gloucester-Hereford Canal completed
	St Martin's Church built
1851	Post Office established on present site
	Woolhope Club founded
1854	Railway reaches Hereford
	Hereford Improvement Act
1859	Plymouth (Christian) Brethren's Barton Hall built
1860	Butter Market opened in High Town
1865	St Paul's Church, Tupsley and St James' Church built
1873	Opening of Museum and Public Library built by Sir James Rankin
	Eignbrook Congregational (United Reform) Church built
1880	St Owen Street Methodist Church built
	Baptist Church built
1882	Some city offices moved to Mansion House
1883	Holy Trinity Church built
1888	H. P. Bulmer's works started in Maylord Street
1889	H. P. Bulmer's works moved to Ryelands Street
1892	Closure of Barton passenger station
1897	Victoria Suspension Bridge built
1899	Electricity generating station opened
1902	Chandos Street Methodist Church built
	Education Act
1904	Town Hall built
	Teachers Training College opened
1907	New west end of cathedral constructed
1908	First city 'bus service
1911	First cinema
1912	Apostolic Church built
1916	Six died in fire at Garrick Theatre

1919	First 'bus service to villages and market towns	1960	22nd Special Air Service Regiment moves to Bradbury Lines
1930	John Masefield, Poet Laureate, received city freedom.	1963	Kemble Theatre demolished
1932	*Hereford Times* becomes only surviving local paper	1966	Greyfriars Bridge and ring road opened
		1969	Art College moves to present site
		1972	Hereford United's famous FA Cup run
1940	County Hospital opened	1973	Nuffield Nursing Home built
1942	Air raid on Hereford, July 27	1974	1972 Local Government Act comes into force and Hereford becomes a District
1953	Henry Wiggin and Co. Ltd. opens Hereford works		
1954	Herefordshire Technical College starts move to present site		

Hereford Youth, 1975, rowing into the city's future.
(Miss Gillian Woodhouse)

142

BIBLIOGRAPHY

ALOH, History of Parish Church of St James, Hereford, Wilson and Phillips, 1910.
ALOH, History of Parish Church of St Nicholas, Hereford, Wilson and Phillips, 1910.
Archaeologia, Vol 37 Pt (i), 1857.
Bannister, A. T., Cathedral Church of Hereford, SPCK, 1924.
Bannister, A. T., Descriptive Catalogue of Mss in Hereford Cathedral, Wilson and Phillips, 1927.
Bannister, A. T., Herefordshire Place Names.
Besse, J., Sufferings of the Quakers, Hinde, 1753.
Birch, W. de G., Cartularium Saxonicum, Whiting, 1893.
Boase, F., Modern English Biography, Cassell, 1965.
Bromyard and District Local History Society Newsletter 7, 1975.
Bury, A., Brian Hatton, 1887-1916, Hereford City, 1973.
Butler, L. A. S., John Gildon of Hereford, Royal Archaeol Inst, 1972.
Capes, W. W., Charters and Records of Hereford Cathedral, Cantilupe Society, 1908.
Carless, W. T., A Short History of Hereford School, 1914.
Charles, B. G. and Emanuel, H. D., Hereford Cathedral Muniments, 3 Vols, National Library of Wales, 1955.
City of Hereford Archaeology Committee, Report I, 1975.
Collins, W., History of Roman Catholic Church of St Francis Xavier, Hereford Times, 1910.
Collins, W., Modern Hereford, Herefordshire Press, 1911.
Colvin, H. M., The History of the King's Works, II, HMSO, 1963.
Couch, A. Quiller, Studies in Literature, Series I, 1920.
Dew, E. W., Index to Registers 1275-1535, Cantilupe Society, 1925.
Dictionary of National Biography.
Duncumb, J., History and Antiquities of the County of Hereford, I, 1804.
Flenley, R., The Register of the Council in the Marches of Wales, 1569-91, Hon Soc Cymmrodorion, 1916.
Fletcher, H. L. V., Herefordshire, Hale, 1948.
Galbraith, V. H. and Tait, J., Herefordshire Domesday, Pipe Roll Soc., 1950.
Herefordshire Natural History, Philosophical Antiquarian and Literary Society, Annual Reports, 1838-45.
Historic Manuscript Commission, 13th Report, Appendix, Pt IV, HMSO, 1892.
Hoskins, W. G., Local History in England, Longmans, 1959.
Jancey, E. M., The Royal Charters of the City of Hereford, City of Hereford, 1973.
Johnson, C. and Croune, H. A., Regesta Regum Anglo-Normanorum, OUP, 1956.
Jones, Joseph, Handbook for Hereford, Jones, 1858.
Jones, John, History of the Baptists in Radnorshire, Elliott Stock, 1895.
Lobel, D., Historic Towns I, Lovell Johns, 1969.
Margary, I. D., Roman Roads in Britain, II, Phoenix, 1957.
Matthews, A. G., Calamy Revised, Oxford, 1934.
Matthews, A. G., Walker Revised, Oxford, 1948.
Mogg, E., Paterson's Roads, Longman, 1822.
Morgan, F. C., Regulations of the City of Hereford, 1557, OUP, 1945.
Page, W. (Ed), VCH Hereford, Vol I, Constable, 1908.
Patterson, D., Description of all the Direct and Principal Cross Roads in Great Britain, Carman, 1771.
Phillott, H. W., Diocesan Histories, Hereford, SPCK, 1888.
Plummer, C., Anglo-Saxon Chronicle, OUP, 1892.
Price, J., City of Hereford, Walker, 1796.
Rahtz, P., Hereford, Current Archaeology, 1969.
Roberts, G. (Ed), City of Hereford Official Guide, 1st Edn, 1969, 4th Edn, 1974.
RCHM, Herefordshire, 3 Vols, HMSO, 1931-34.
Shoesmith, R., The City of Hereford Archaeology and Development, Wemrac, 1974.
Slocombe, I. M. (Ed), Studies in the History of Hereford, WEA Univ of Birmingham, 1967.
Smith, L. Toulmin, Leland's Itinerary in Wales, Bell, 1906.
Stanford, S. C., Credenhill, Herefordshire, Royal Archaeol Inst, 1971.
Testa de Nevill c 1327, Record Commission, 1807.
Traherne, Thomas, Centuries, Poems and Thanksgivings.
Traherne, Thomas, Poems of Felicity.
Whitlock, D., Anglo-Saxon Wills, CUP, 1920.
Wightman, W. E., The Lacy Family in England and Normandy, 1066-1194, OUP, 1966.
Williamson, J., 50 Years at Edgar Street, Hereford Printing Co, 1974.
Woolhope Club, Herefordshire, BPC, 1954.
Woolhope Naturalists' Field Club Transactions, 1851-1974.
Calendar Close Rolls.
Calendar Inquisitions Miscellaneous.
Calendar Liberate Rolls.
Calendar Papal Letters.
Calendar Patent Rolls.
Calendar State Papers Domestic, Elizabeth.
Catalogue Ancient Deeds.
Pipe Rolls, Pipe Roll Society.
Directories:
    Jakeman and Carver, Herefordshire, 1890.
    Kelly's, Hereford, 1939.
    Kelly's, Herefordshire, 1900, 1905, 1909, 1913, 1934, 1937, 1941.
    Lascelles and Co, Herefordshire, 1851.
    Littlebury, Hereford, 1867, 1876.
    Pigot, J. and Co, Hereford, 1830, 1835.
    Robson, London and the Western Counties, 1840.
    Slater, Hereford, 1850, 1859.
    Universal British, 1793.

Index

Subscribers

Presentation copies

1 **Hereford District Council**
2 **County Council of Hereford & Worcester**
3 **F. C. Morgan, FSA, FLA, Hon. MA**
4 **Cllr M. Prendergast**
5 **The Bishop of Hereford**
6 **Hereford College of Art**
7 **County Record Office, Hereford**
8 **The Hereford Library**

9 Stephen Jones
10 Mike Spencer
11 Jim and Muriel Tonkin
12 Clive Birch
13 J. S. & M. Keely
14 Mrs M. Evans
15 J. D. Starbuck
16 R. C. & V. Perry
17 } C. E. Attfield
18
19 S. L. Beaumont
20 C. J. Lloyd
21 Mrs R. Bradshaw
22 R. H. Bulmer
23 James Gerald
   Calderbank
24 N. S. Carter, MRCVS
25 A. M. Eagling
26 Robert E. Earl
27 Robert Michael Green
28 Miss Evelyn M. Horne
29 A. L. Moir
30 } Alan Morris
31
32 Mrs Parker
33 H. Pebody
34 Derek T. Preece
35 D. Price
36 Percy Pritchard
37 N. C. Reeves
38 D. C. Roberts
39 Mrs L. M. Sheldrake
40 Ron Shoesmith
41 Miss M. Spurway
42 Norman Bricknell
43 Basil Butcher
44 Ernest John Leslie Cole
45 V. H. Coleman
46 D. J. Collins
47 H. J. Dance
48 S. A. Davis
49 A. N. Dees
50 Maj R. N. L. Denyer, RA
51 } Dr A. W. Langford
52
53 Group Captain J. B.
   Lewis
54 T. A. Neal
55 Robert Page
56 } Mrs E. G. Peters
57

58 Graham Sprackling
59 Uplands Teachers'
   Centre
60 } B. Bulmer
61
62
63 } Gillian Bulmer
64
65 G. C. Davies
66 Mrs R. B. Haig
67 F. A. Leeds
68
69 } C. Marshall
70
71 Herbert J. Powell
72 Manley Power
73 Michael and Yvonne
   Ray
74 M. Thompson
75 E. M. Wheeldon
76 W. H. D. Wince
77 } Mrs A. D. Brian
78
79 A. Leslie Charles
80 Philip Charleton
81 Miss Lily F. Chitty,
   OBE, MA, FSA
82 G. W. E. Farrow
83 W. E. Griffiths
84 H. J. Lloyd Johnes,
   OBE, TD, LLD, FSA
85 Mrs R. D. E. E. Mills
86 Mrs Elizabeth
   Richardson
87 John Taylor
88 B. F. Voss
89 I. O. Capper
90 } C. J. Christmas
91
92 A. T. G. Garnett
93 Miss E. McQuillan
94 Mrs A. M. A. Phillips
95 } I. K. Porter
96
97 G. B. Jones
98 Miss J. R. Davies
99 M. A. Faraday
100 Winifred M. Prosser
101 Dr S. C. Stanford
102 Miss G. A. Francis
103 I. W. R. Spriggs

104 Mrs K. J. Davies
105 N. R. Dove, BSc, AMA
106 A. W. Branston
107 Nancy M. Elliott
108 C. C. Harley
109 Miss V. Organ
110 D. A. Whitehead
111 Mrs M. G. Hole
112 } P. N. D. Porter
113
114 N. H. Peabody
115 G. W. Thomas
116 G. A. Millman
117 R. S. Francis
118 John Caine
119 Lord Croft
120 D. M. R. Pryce
121 G. P. Smart
122 A. P. Begg
123 James Borthwick
124 George Charnock
125 C. T. C. Davies
126 Miss J. Godfrey-Merrick
127 P. J. Jones
128 Frank Noble
129 G. Wilkins
130 F. I. Williams
131 George and Marjorie
   Bannard
132 Miss S. K. Parry
133 Miss C. M. Parry
134 H. A. Hall
135 Mrs M. E. Hunt
136 Mr & Mrs C. T. O.
   Prosser
137 J. B. Bach
138 John Beesley
139 J. E. Dunn
140 Linda Bull
141 Mrs Laura E. Griffiths
142 J. J. Rees
143 I. Whittal-Williams
144 J. L. Everett
145 H. R. & J. R.
   Griffiths
146 Sir Alfred Nicholas,
   CBE, LLD
147 Miss D. E. Whitefoot
148 Mrs E. Edinborough
149 Peter F. Wyndham
   Pember

150 Mr & Mrs F. C. Buckle
151 Mrs Sonia Croasdell
152 Dr Eric A. Gee, FSA
153 Christopher John Dunn,
   BA, Dip Th
154 H. J. Dance
155 Extramural Librarian,
   University of
   Birmingham
156
157 } R. M. Humphreys
158
159 Denis Lambin
160 M. P. West
161 Philip John Wride
162 Joan M. Davidson
163 Miss L. F. Goodwin
164 C. S. Grisman
165 Howard Jones
166 D. C. Hands
167 J. E. Hardwick
168 Mrs M. Whitwell
169 K. W. and R. M.
   Benton
170 Janet and John Gaunt
171 Wg Cdr A. M. Gill,
   OBE, DFC, AFRScS,
   MIPM, BMIM
172 Mrs D. F. Griffiths
173 A. L. Rutherford
174 Dr W. H. J. Baker
175 Gary Davies
176 K. T. Dolling
177 Miss P. A. Fenner
178 John and Doreen Fryer
179 M. H. A. McMichael
180 Mrs D. R. Rees
181 Mr & Mrs R. H.
   Sidwick
182 D. W. A. Morgan
183 Roy H. Badman
184 Mr & Mrs T. G.
   Richardson
185 Marian E. Wiles
186 Mrs R. Kirk-Owen
187 Mrs J. Le Prevost
188 F. Morris
189 Norah Walker
190 Shropshire County
   Library
191 D. Nicholas

192	J. H. Wickers	327	Graham Bunting	
193	J. M. Acheson	328	Mr & Mrs Craig	
194	Mary Elliott and		Naudain	
	Sheila Wenham	329	Mrs Richard Sudworth	
195	B. Watkins	330	R. F. Green	

192   J. H. Wickers
193   J. M. Acheson
194   Mary Elliott and
        Sheila Wenham
195   B. Watkins
196   M. Milburn
197   Hugh Thomas
198   G. E. Barrett
199 ⎱ Martin Opie, B.Arch,
200 ⎰ RIBA, MCD, MRTPI
201   Richard Tamplin
202   R. D. Willmot
203   Mr & Mrs P. J.
        Bradburn
204   Joan White
205   Mike Prendergast
206   Roger Morgan
207   F. E. Powell
208   Leo Brace
209   E. Olga Zakrzewski
210   B. W. Evans, BA
211   M. J. Brett Young
212   H. G. Culliss
213   Ernle Gilbert
214   Mrs English
215   Noreen and Bryan
        Keely
216   Mrs R. S. Griffin
217   B. J. Whitehouse
218   B. W. Davies
219   B. W. Harris
220   G. E. Forrest
221   Mrs J. I. Rutherford
222   B. G. Cooke
223   R. Parrott
224   Robert W. Price
225   Mrs S. A. Morrill
226   Julie Buckle
227   Mrs L. N. Alloway
228   Mrs O. Cleak
229   James Bendle
230   Don Williams
231   M. H. Heroman
232   Miles W. Keen
233   Mrs E. E. J. Davidson
234   Miss J. Rogers
235   The Phillipps Librarian
236   Christine Sadler
237   Rev J. D. Blaney
238   R. V. D. Middleton
239   M. J. P. McCarthy
240   E. H. Clark
241   W. J. Hart
242   Mr & Mrs H. Disley
243   Miss S. E. S. Griffiths
244   D. G. Cullom
245   M. E. Morton Lloyd
246   The Librarian,
        Herefordshire
        Technical College
247   G. Brookes
248   D. Jenner
249 ⎱ Hereford and
to   ⎰ Worcester County
309   Libraries
310   Mrs A. M. Leonard
311   Miss A. M. Jones
312   Mr & Mrs R. M. Dakin
313   Mrs E. Farrington
314   R. C. B. Oliver
315   A. N. Morrison
316 ⎱
317 ⎬ T. W. Barnes
318 ⎰
319   Miss L. Lawrence
320   Mrs Antoinette Powell
321   M. E. Webster
322   Andrew Gray
323   Sally Julia Lewis
324   J. H. Shann
325   Miss M. Slatter
326   P. G. Williams

327   Graham Bunting
328   Mr & Mrs Craig
        Naudain
329   Mrs Richard Sudworth
330   R. F. Green
331   L. Faulkes
332   Mrs J. Slade
333   B. A. Loughman
334   Miss J. D. Pethybridge
335   Miss Eva Handley
336   P. L. Bodger
337   G. Newton-Sealey
338   A. B. Turner
339   T. Batho
340   C. R. Colley
341   J. A. Eggleston
342   W. D. Matthews
343   B. V. C. Stone
344   D. A. Botterill
345   Mrs S. M. Brown
346   Miss A. S. Ford
347   David Yeld
348   R. Hargest
349   Stuart Ruffe
350   Nicholas Handoll
351   Eunice Davies
352   Emily Midwinter
353   John Lynne-Brook
354   David J. Greenhalf
355   Dr M. H. K. Haggie
356   Mrs Lynda Vaughan
357   Brian Vaughan
358   J. R. Setterfield
359   Mrs M. K. Cox
360   J. N. Taylor
361   H. W. Broome
362   Mr & Mrs Basil
        Davidson
363   Mrs M. E. Wade
364   A. Hesten
365   Mr & Mrs C. Shields
366   Mrs Nancy K. M. S.
        Hancorn
367   Mary Martin
368   J. M. Heygate
369   T. W. Wellington
370   A. L. Dickinson
371   Miss J. D. Fletcher
372   A. E. Merritt
373   Peter Clinton
374   M. J. P. H. Roche
375   Miss P. M. Wilks
376   Mrs B. D. Kelly
377   A. Thomas
378   J. W. Urwin
379   R. A. Perks
380   R. J. Williams
381   J. M. Williams
382   Morley L. Smith
383   R. J. Courtney
384   Mrs E. M. Rees
385   S. Bodenham
386   Mrs D. M. Watkins
387   N. Moss
388   Ruth Elizabeth Millard
389   Roy Massey
390   E. E. Brooks
391   A. Parish
392   M. S. Richards
393   Rebecca F. Hill
394   Bromyard District Local
        History Society
395   Miss E. D. Pearson
396   Joy Hopkins
397   A. C. Barlow
398 ⎱ University of Leicester
399 ⎰ Library
400   Miss J. Constance Purser
401   The White House
        Helpers Group
402   Leominster District
        Council

403 ⎱ Miss P. A. Farr
404 ⎰
405   Mrs M. Frankenburg
406   Mrs Joan Lane
407   L. P. Moore
408   Alan Stewart
409   H. S. Widgery
410   Mrs R. H. Cooke
411   Mr & Mrs Edgar
        Godwin
412   Robert J. Tolley,
        RIBA
413   Mrs M. Bate
414   Jane Taylor
415   A. H. Bedding
416   Gladys Irene Sarah
        Marriott
417   Mr & Mrs C. R. Garfitt
418   Dr G. Barnes
419   G. Ivor Williams
420   R. G. Schafer
421   Minnie Edwards
422   Mr & Mrs Basil
        Davidson
423   Mrs Gwyneth Green
424   William A. Blake
425   D. Williams
426   Mrs A. Telford
427   Leominster Historical
        Society
428   Mrs G. C. Warren
429   Mrs W. Leeds
430   Mrs V. M. Rosser
431   Mrs P. H. Lees-Smith
432 ⎱ T. H. Jay
433 ⎰
434   Mr & Mrs P. C.
        Cruttenden
435   F. M. Kendrick
436   Fitzroy E. Reynolds
437   Peter Thomson
438   Mrs Sarah T. Egbert
439   Mervyn Jones
440   Miss Janette Smout
441   K. L. Paulo
442 ⎱ Mrs P. W. Watkins
443 ⎰
444   Claire Penford
445   Mrs Betty Cooper
446   A. C. Green
447   M. R. J. Perrott
448   Leslie Edward Hyde
449   Mrs J. O'Donnell
450   Robert Deeley
451   S. W. Davies
452   Miss S. G. Dunne
453   Mrs J. McCulloch
454   P. G. Jones
455   Mrs M. U. Jones
456   Mr & Mrs J. Hyde
457   Wigmore Primary
        School
458   Inett Homes
459   M. A. Jones
460 ⎱ Mrs Midwood
461 ⎰
462   John Simons
463   Hereford and
        Worcester County
        Museum
464   Mrs B. G. Bryer
465   Mrs E. M. Williams
466   Brian William Mason
467   R. N. Blackburne
468   Miss L. B. Britton
469   Jeremy Soulsby
470   Mrs W. C. Smith
471   Mrs U. Fitzgerald
472   Mrs G. A. Main
473   Trevor H. A. Ely
474   Norman Ward
475   W. Hammond

476   Rodney H. Bennett
477   E. G. Shankie
478   Fiona Nicol
479   T. Shellis
480   Mrs Ursula Marion
        Mills
481   D. Williams
482   Mrs L. I. Pugh
483   P. N. Fisher, MA
484   Mr & Mrs L. A. K.
        Harris
485   N. P. Morris
486   R. J. H. Hill
487   Mrs M. H. Holliday
488   Kenneth Truman
489   D. Jukes
490   Mrs E. J. Ingram
491   J. M. Williams
492   S. C. Hewitt
493   K. Farnes
494   Mrs D. E. Phillips
495   Alan Mifflin
496   Jillian B. Ward
497   The Ewias Historical
        and Archaeological
        Society
498   Mr & Mrs E. Browning
499   Miss J. M. Houston
500   Dewi Francis Thomas,
        BA
501   Christopher Over
502   City of Hereford
        Tourist Information
        Centre
503   Mrs G. B. Leppard
504   M. Lane
505   Raymond W. Birch,
        CBE
506   G. J. Roberts
507   Dr R. S. Hall
508   Miss J. E. Davies
509   Arthur Dennis
        Edmunds
510   J. Harnden
511   E. R. Saunders
512   Marjorie Blossett
513   A. J. W. Hall
514   T. J. Handley
515   H. Webster, MBE
516   Haywood High School
517   Miss Muriel Jones
518   H. K. Hill
519   Mrs Druscilla Gordon-
        Pedersen
520   C. J. Sansom
521   Godfrey C. Davies
522 ⎱ Miss F. M. Taylor
523 ⎰
524   Simon McGurk
525   Mrs J. C. Price
526   Mrs G. M. Murray
527   Wigmore High School
528   Charles Woolf
529   Miss J. F. Manning
530   Mrs P. A. Stansbury
531   Mrs Pennie Townsend
532   Peter and Ann Davey
533   S. C. Jones
534   Mrs M. Tennant
535   G. E. Jenkins
536   L. R. Sadler
537   P. W. Baker
538 ⎱ R. T. Collins
539 ⎰
540   Eric T. Price
541   M. T. Anderson
542   Ramsay St. George
543   John and Judy Geary
544   Mrs L. Phillips
545   G. J. Baker
546   Elfriede Lustig
547   P. G. Worthing

548	R. N. Gardiner	591	D. B. Powell	634	F. S. Matthews	675	H. R. Jenman
549	B. R. Stephenson	592	H. G. Pitt	635	M. A. W. Vale	676	R. Davies
550	Mrs E. F. De Grey	593	Mrs H. D. Smith	636	E. W. Baynham	677	S. W. Smith
551	Mrs George Edward Breen	594	J. E. Chadd	637	A. H. Weale	678	Mrs Elizabeth W. Tonkin
552	Major F. M. Symonds	595	W. A. Chadd	638	F. C. Morgan	679	Kenneth and Audrey Tonkin
553	Arthur W. Jenkins	596	W. J. Kendal	639	A. Baugh		
554	Mrs F. A. Joorabchiam	597	Betty L. Howls	640	E. L. Lambert	680	Peter Tonkin
555	Birmingham Public Libraries	598 599	} Sir Michael Cambell	641	John C. Russell	681	Nigel Tonkin
				642	Miss Ann Sandford	682	J. S. & E. M. George
556	A. J. Weston	600 601	} David Llewellyn	643	Mr & Mrs M. Daly	683	Stephen C. Millett
557	Miss T. G. Matthews			644	The Genealogical Society of the Church of the Latter Day Saints	684	Woolhope Naturalists Field Club
558	D. M. Fowler	602	Charles and Betty Wegg-Prosser				
559	A. P. Drabble	603	Catering Services Ltd	645	Mr & Mrs A. Woodhouse	685	R. H. Beddoes
560 561	} R. N. Clifford	604	S. E. Roberts			686	Mrs G. Hoskins
		605	Miss J. D. Pethybridge	646	Roger Thomas	687	C. T. Bishop & Son Ltd
562	Miss Helen Johnson	606	G. W. Smith	647	Stephen and Vicki Wegg-Prosser		
563	J. L. Hackman	607	R. Haworth			688	R. E. Clarke
564	D. J. Brooke	608	W. H. Phillips	648	Mrs C. A. Bennett	689	Martin E. Speight
565	Mrs M. L. Glenister	609	Mrs E. H. Cunningham	649	Angela Mary Cound	690	Miss C. Speight
566	A. B. Sherratt	610	Rex Cyril Jordan	650	A. J. Dewar	691	P. W. Pritchard
567	Thomas Griffiths	611	Miss J. E. Davies	651	Mrs Muriel Cundale	692	Alan C. Price
568	G. B. Jones	612	Mrs J. A. G. Hart	652	W. A. Gardiner	693	C. J. Williams
569	G. C. Cartwright	613	Herbert Simmons	653	M. R. Parry	694	Frank Goddard
570	Reginald Frank Dawe	614	R. J. McCoy	654	Julia Anne Cound	695	Mrs E. A. Howarth
571	R. W. Edgar	615	V. C. Cooke	655	Mrs A. J. Paske	696	Mrs J. M. Bentley-Taylor
572	Mrs B. Morris	616	D. W. Davies	656	Mrs D. Westoby		
573	C. J. C. Renton	617	Hereford High School for Girls	657	A. J. Hughes	697	A. E. Alakija
574	D. H. Snell			658	The Sibbicks	698	Edward G. Taylor
575	M. Pauly	618	Stephen R. Bainbridge	659	Mrs E. Brazier	699	Mr & Mrs E. Ward
576	Dr & Mrs Edwin Course	619	T. H. Burn	660	P. J. G. Mort	700	Marjorie Cunningham
		620	Mr & Mrs P. C. Freeman	661	Miss V. Southorn	701	Miss R. E. Hickling
577	David Warburton			662	Peter Dolan	702	Valerie C. Baskwill
578	J. H. Robinson	621	R. A. C. Blanchard	663	Michael Dolan	703	Malcolm Read
579	Mrs E. M. McNeil	622	J. Dickson	664	Mrs J. R. Pullen	704	David Read
580	W. H. Godding	623	Peter Chard	665	Miss J. Winter	705	F. R. Smith
581	Miss P. F. Dawson	624	Tom Lloyd	666	C. J. & G. A. Claypole	706 707 708 709	} Mrs M. H. Goode
582	Peter S. Hill	625	Maureen A. Hind	667	Mrs A. D. Baskerville		
583	Mrs M. M. Cooper	626	H. J. Stephenson	668	G. E. Morris		
584	J. G. Sweetman	627	Mrs P. Broadbent	669	Mr & Mrs F. G. Salter		
585	A. Briffett	628	R. A. Sewell	670	Eleanor M. E. Daniels	710	J. R. Alcock
586	E. Henry Dorrell	629	Miss J. Aingel	671 672	} Hereford College of Education		
587	Mrs E. M. Peach	630	Mrs K. Watkins				
588	P. W. Francis	631	Dr Roy Strong	673	Hereford College of Art		
589	M. A. Jackson-Dooley	632	D. A. Apperly	674	Rev E. Ward, AKC, FSA Scot.		
590	A. V. Ryder	633	B. W. Waters				

Remaining names unlisted.

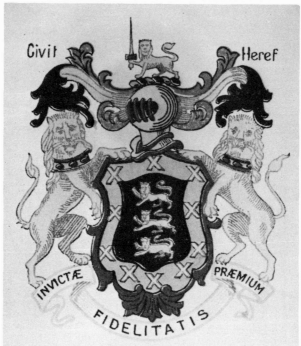

Arms granted in 1645.

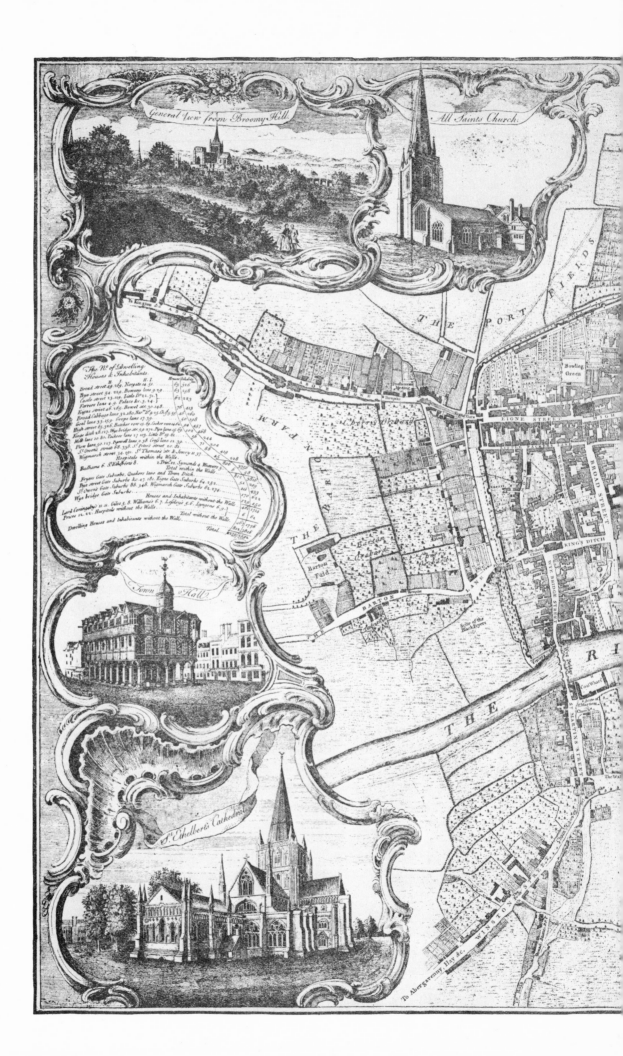

General View from Broomy Hill.

All Saints Church.

Town Hall.

St. Ethelbert's Cathedral.